THE N
FAV
COMI

THE NATION'S FAVOURITE COMIC POEMS

—◇—

FOREWORD BY
GRIFF RHYS JONES

BBC
BOOKS

1 3 5 7 9 10 8 6 4 2

First published in 1998. This edition first published 2008.

Published by BBC Books, an imprint of Ebury Publishing.
A Random House Group Company

The Random House Group Limited Reg. No. 954009

Addresses for companies within the Random House Group
can be found at www.randomhouse.co.uk

A CIP catalogue record for this book is available
from the British Library.

ISBN 978 1 846 07648 0

The Random House Group Limited supports the Forest
Stewardship Council (FSC), the leading international forest
certification organization. All our titles that are printed on
Greenpeace approved FSC certified paper carry the FSC logo.
Our paper procurement policy can be found at
www.rbooks.co.uk/environment

Printed and bound in Great Britain by
CPI Cox & Wyman, Reading, RG1 8EX

CONTENTS

— ◇ —

– Contents –

– Contents –

FOREWORD BY GRIFF RHYS JONES

— ◇ —

What is a comic poem? How do you decide? What criteria could you possibly employ? Well, soon the nation will decide and, to help you in your choice, I have made up my own selection of likely candidates. It wasn't easy because, alas, not all comic poems are funny, particularly those that try to be. But, as you wander through this collection, I hope you'll be tickled. You will also find that poets high and low, famous, great even, have managed to write some pretty funny stuff on the side, even if our leading contributor is, nonetheless, Anon.

Happily, there is a type of writer who, if often shown the door in other anthologies, has the run of the house here. These are the masters of their craft, the wizards of the unexpected rhyme: the Comic Poets. Perhaps it was the freedom to write nonsense, inflicted so successfully on children by Edward Lear and Lewis Carroll, that opened the way to the gloriously silly stuff. (Although I suspect that *Punch* had a lot to do with it.) Anyway, it is good to see those old nags Hilaire Belloc and Harry Graham coming round the track again. The nursery mood may not be very elevating, but it can be pretty funny.

One of my personal favourites is this little verse by the American wit Gelett Burgess, which was first published in the 1890s.

> I never saw a Purple Cow,
> I never hope to see one;
> But I can tell you, anyhow,
> I'd rather see than be one.

Some years later he wrote again:

> Ah yes! I wrote the 'Purple Cow'–
> I'm Sorry, now, I Wrote it!
> But I can Tell you, Anyhow,
> I'll Kill you if you Quote it!

Poor man. For all I know he designed lunatic asylums or walked backwards to the North Pole. Today all that survives of his verse is this piece of doggerel. I suppose he would have been mortified to find it still doing the rounds.

Mind you, all good jokes are a sort of poetry, aren't they? Gagsmiths know the value of the *mot juste*, the necessity of rhythm and, er, of course, that timing thing. It should come as no surprise that poetry returns the compliment. Puns, wordplay, hidden meanings and the wrong-footing of cherished notions: it's the very stuff of verse. But jokes eventually die off. Funny poems go on. (On and on, some of them. Lewis Carroll could prolong the hilarity through many a now-forgotten stanza.)

I once recited Robert Service's stirring 'The Cremation of Sam McGee' (not short, but sublime) at a fund-raising event and a woman came up to me afterwards. She voluntarily 'did' half of 'The Shooting of Dan McGrew' while I queued for my coat, and continued while I walked down a flight of steps and got into my car. She may be doing it still, for all I know. People *will* carry around rhyming saws and useful epithets for the purpose of bringing them up at appropriate moments. Some of them are here. If you lack these essentials to good conversation, feel free to pinch a few.

Mind you, if you are going to plagiarize, it is as well to remember that brevity is the soul of other people's wit. For my own purposes, I find Sir Walter Raleigh very useful. He wrote a series of verse observations to an artist friend, on postcards. (This is a later Walter Raleigh, by the way. Not the one with the inflatable short trousers and the potatoes.)

> I wish I loved the Human Race;
> I wished I loved its silly face; . . .
> And when I'm introduced to one
> I wish I thought *What Jolly Fun*!

Cynics often join me in cackling at this. 'It sums it all up, eh?' Though to be fair, it was written about some sorry-looking old trout at a garden party and was meant as criticism. Anyway, my point is I always edit the middle couplet out for efficiency. You can find the full version on page 141.

It is a challenge to try to be profound and laugh-out-loud funny at the same time. This is why poets of wit, invention and style, like John Donne and Alexander Pope, at whom professors may chortle and teachers hoot, are minimally represented in this anthology.

It is also a pity that certain poets so deeply profound as to be utterly asinine are not here either. Is there anything in the whole of literature more amusing than William Wordsworth struggling to elevate the commonplace:

> Spade! With which Wilkinson hath tilled his lands.
> 'To the Spade of a Friend'

Or how about this, from one Lillian Curtis, who wrote, in all seriousness:

> I loved the gentle girl,
> But oh, I heaved a sigh,
> When first she told me she could see
> Out of only one eye.

A victim of the measles, apparently. But these are bad poems which are unintentionally funny, and they need their own collection. (*The Nation's Favourite Terrible Poems* perhaps?)

There is also a lot of recent writing here. After all, the nation's favourite modern poem was a funny one. 'Warning' by Jenny Joseph is naturally in the running again. But so are poems by Wendy Cope, Pam Ayres, Roger McGough and Roald Dahl. So are ones by John Hegley and E.J. Thribb, the mythical contributor to *Private Eye*.

Poets these days have all become sit-down comedians. Almost everybody from Allen Ginsberg to Brian Patten seems to get off on the 'wry look at the way we live now'.

But the funniest poem? Well, we shall have to wait until the votes are counted. As old television schedulers say: 'There's no accounting for public taste.' And there are some rum doings here.

Altogether, however, this is a testament to the power of poetry to move us in the chest-heaving sort of way. (Laughter and tears, they're never far apart, are they, governor? Is there a more moving love poem in the English language than 'The Courtship of the Yonghy-Bonghy-Bò'?) Comic poems, I vow, are a great popular means of expression. You only have to sit in the lavatories at King's Cross station to understand that. It will be fascinating to see what gets the popular vote on the night.

Remembered, half-remembered, beloved, cherished or written on tea towels, here are some of my favourite comic poems.

JOHN AGARD

COFFEE IN HEAVEN

You'll be greeted
by a nice cup of coffee
when you get to heaven
and strains of angelic harmony.

But wouldn't you be devastated
if they only serve decaffeinated
while from the percolators of hell

your soul was assaulted
by Satan's fresh espresso smell?

ALLAN AHLBERG 1938–

PLEASE MRS BUTLER

Please Mrs Butler
This boy Derek Drew
Keeps copying my work, Miss.
What shall I do?

Go and sit in the hall, dear.
Go and sit in the sink.
Take your books on the roof, my lamb.
Do whatever you think.

Please Mrs Butler
This boy Derek Drew
Keeps taking my rubber, Miss.
What shall I do?

Keep it in your hand, dear.
Hide it up your vest.
Swallow it if you like, my love.
Do what you think best.

Please Mrs Butler
This boy Derek Drew
Keeps calling me rude names, Miss.
What shall I do?

Lock yourself in the cupboard, dear.
Run away to sea.
Do whatever you can, my flower.
But *don't ask me!*

ANON

ON MARY ANN

Mary Ann has gone to rest,
Safe at last on Abraham's breast,
Which may be nuts for Mary Ann,
But is certainly rough on Abraham.

ANON

ON A TIRED HOUSEWIFE

Here lies a poor woman who was always tired,
She lived in a house where help wasn't hired:
Her last words on earth were: 'Dear friends, I am going
To where there's no cooking, or washing, or sewing,
For everything there is exact to my wishes,
For where they don't eat there's no washing of dishes.
I'll be where loud anthems will always be ringing,
But having no voice I'll be quit of the singing.
Don't mourn for me now, don't mourn for me never,
I am going to do nothing for ever and ever.'

ANON

SPRING IN THE BRONX

Spring is sprung,
Duh grass is riz
I wonder where dem boidies is.

Duh little boids is on duh wing –
But dat's absoid:
Duh little wing is on duh boid.

ANON
———

THE CRIMES OF LIZZIE BORDEN

Lizzie Borden with an axe,
Hit her father forty whacks,
When she saw what she had done,
She hit her mother forty-one.

ANON

I HAVE A GENTLE COCK

I have a gentle cock,
Croweth me day:
He doth me risen erly
My matins for to say.

I have a gentle cock,
Comen he is of gret:
His comb is of red coral,
His tail is of jet.

I have a gentle cock,
Comen he is of kinde:
His comb is of red coral,
His tail is of inde.

His legges ben of asor,
So gentle and so smale;
His spores arn of silver whit
Into the wortewale.

His eynen arn of cristal,
Loken all in aumber:
And every night he percheth him
In mine ladye's chaumber.

ANON

SHE WAS POOR BUT SHE WAS HONEST

She was poor, but she was honest,
    Victim of the squire's whim:
First he loved her, then he left her,
    And she lost her honest name.

Then she ran away to London,
    For to hide her grief and shame;
There she met another squire,
    And she lost her name again.

See her riding in her carriage,
    In the Park and all so gay:
All the nibs and nobby persons
    Come to pass the time of day.

See the little old-world village
    Where her aged parents live,
Drinking the champagne she sends them;
    But they never can forgive.

In the rich man's arms she flutters,
    Like a bird with broken wing:
First he loved her, then he left her,
    And she hasn't got a ring.

See him in the splendid mansion,
    Entertaining with the best,
While the girl that he has ruined,
    Entertains a sordid guest.

See him in the House of Commons,
    Making laws to put down crime,
While the victim of his passions
    Trails her way through mud and slime.

Standing on the bridge at midnight,
    She says: 'Farewell, blighted Love.'
There's a scream, a splash – Good Heavens!
    What is she a-doing of?

Then they drag her from the river,
    Water from her clothes they wrang,
For they thought that she was drownded;
    But the corpse got up and sang:

'It's the same the whole world over;
    It's the poor that gets the blame,
It's the rich that gets the pleasure.
    Isn't it a blooming shame?'

ANON
———

IF ALL THE WORLD WERE PAPER

If all the world were paper,
  And all the sea were ink,
If all the trees were bread and cheese,
  How should we do for drink?

If all the world were sand O,
  Oh then what should we lack O,
If as they say there were no clay,
  How should we take tobacco?

If all our vessels ran-a,
  If none but had a crack-a,
If Spanish apes ate all the grapes,
  How should we do for sack-a?

If all the world were men,
  And men lived all in trenches,
And there were none but we alone,
  How should we do for wenches?

If friars had no bald pates,
  Nor nuns had no dark cloisters,
If all the seas were beans and peas,
  How should we do for oysters?

If there had been no projects,
  Nor none that did great wrongs,
If fiddlers shall turn players all,
  How should we do for songs?

If all things were eternal,
  And nothing their end bringing,
If this should be, then how should we
  Here make an end of singing?

ANON

PEAS

I always eat peas with honey,
I've done it all my life,
They do taste kind of funny,
But it keeps them on the knife.

ANON

THE PIG

It was an evening in November,
As I very well remember,
I was strolling down the street in drunken pride,
But my knees were all a-flutter,
And I landed in the gutter
And a pig came up and lay down by my side.

Yes, I lay there in the gutter
Thinking thoughts I could not utter,
When a colleen passing by did softly say
'You can tell a man who boozes
By the company he chooses' –
And the pig got up and slowly walked away.

W. H. AUDEN 1907–73

GIVE ME A DOCTOR

Give me a doctor partridge-plump,
Short in the leg and broad in the rump,
An endomorph with gentle hands
Who'll never make absurd demands
That I abandon all my vices
Nor pull a long face in a crisis,
But with a twinkle in his eye
Will tell me that I have to die.

W. H. AUDEN 1907–73

NOTE ON INTELLECTUALS

To the man-in-the-street, who, I'm sorry to say
   Is a keen observer of life,
The word Intellectual suggests straight away
   A man who's untrue to his wife.

PAM AYRES 1947–

SLING ANOTHER CHAIR LEG ON THE FIRE, MOTHER

Sling another chair leg on the fire, Mother,
Pull your orange box up to the blaze,
Hold your poor old mittens out and warm them
In these inflationary days.
Sink your teeth into that dripping sandwich,
Flick the telly on to channel nine,
And if we get the sound without the picture,
Well, I'll kick it in the kidneys, one more time.

Come with me out to the empty garage,
We haven't been there for a week or more,
We'll bow our heads and gaze in silent homage
At the spots of oil upon the floor.
We'll think of when we had a motor car there,
Which used to take us out in rain or shine,
Before the price of petrol went beyond us,
And we'll make believe we kept it, one more time.

Fling another sausage in the pan, Mother!
We'll laugh away our worries and our cares,
But we'll never get a doctor after hours, Mother,
So for God's sake don't go falling down the stairs.
Toss another lentil in the soup, Mother!
And serve it up before the News at nine,
And if the GPO detector spots us,
Make believe we've got a licence, one more time.

There was a time we'd booked up for Ibiza,
We'd bought the suntan lotion and the clothes,
But we never got beyond the travel agent,
'Cause Court Line organised the one we chose.
So knock the clouds of dust from off the brochure,
Wipe the 40-watt bulb free of grime,
Turn the dog-eared pages to Ibiza,
And we'll make believe we got there, one more time.

Pass me the hatchet and the axe, Mother!
Wipe away that sad and anxious frown,
What with these inflationary spirals,
It's *nice* to see the table falling down.
Your poor old shins will soon be good and mottled,
Once the flames get round that teak veneer,
And in the ring of warm and dancing firelight,
We'll smile and wish each other: Happy New Year.

PAM AYRES 1947–

OH, I WISH I'D LOOKED AFTER ME TEETH

Oh, I wish I'd looked after me teeth,
  And spotted the perils beneath
All the toffees I chewed,
  And the sweet sticky food.
Oh, I wish I'd looked after me teeth.

I wish I'd been that much more willin'
  When I had more tooth there than fillin'
To give up gobstoppers,
  From respect to me choppers,
And to buy something else with me shillin'.

When I think of the lollies I licked
  And the liquorice allsorts I picked,
Sherbet dabs, big and little,
  All that hard peanut brittle,
My conscience gets horribly pricked.

My mother, she told me no end,
  'If you got a tooth, you got a friend.'
I was young then, and careless,
  My toothbrush was hairless,
I never had much time to spend.

Oh I showed them the toothpaste all right,
  I flashed it about late at night,
But up-and-down brushin'
  And pokin' and fussin'
Didn't seem worth the time – I could bite!

If I'd known I was paving the way
     To cavities, caps and decay,
The murder of fillin's,
     Injections and drillin's,
I'd have thrown all me sherbet away.

So I lay in the old dentist's chair,
     And I gaze up his nose in despair,
And his drill it do whine
     In these molars of mine.
'Two amalgam,' he'll say, 'for in there.'

How I laughed at my mother's false teeth,
     As they foamed in the waters beneath.
But now comes the reckonin'
     It's *me* they are beckonin'
Oh, I *wish* I'd looked after me teeth.

PATRICK BARRINGTON 1908–90

I HAD A DUCK-BILLED PLATYPUS

I had a duck-billed platypus when I was up at Trinity,
With whom I soon discovered a remarkable affinity.
He used to live in lodgings with myself and Arthur Purvis,
And we all went up together for the Diplomatic Service.
I had a certain confidence, I own, in his ability,
He mastered all the subjects with remarkable facility;
And Purvis, though more dubious, agreed that he was clever,
But no one else imagined he had any chance whatever.
I failed to pass the interview, the Board with wry grimaces
Took exception to my boots and then objected to my braces,
And Purvis too was failed by an intolerant examiner
Who said he had his doubts as to his sock-suspenders' stamina.
The bitterness of failure was considerably mollified,
However, by the ease with which our platypus had qualified.
The wisdom of the choice, it soon appeared, was undeniable;
There never was a diplomat more thoroughly reliable.
He never made rash statements his enemies might hold him to,
He never stated anything, for no one ever told him to,
And soon he was appointed, so correct was his behaviour,
Our Minister (without Portfolio) to Trans-Moravia.
My friend was loved and honoured from the Andes to Esthonia,
He soon achieved a pact between Peru and Patagonia,
He never vexed the Russians nor offended the Rumanians,
He pacified the Letts and yet appeased the Lithuanians,
Won approval from his masters down in Downing Street
  so wholly, O,
He was soon to be rewarded with the grant of a Portfolio.

When, on the Anniversary of Greek Emancipation,
Alas! He laid an egg in the Bulgarian Legation.
This untoward occurrence caused unheard-of repercussions,
Giving rise to epidemics of sword-clanking in the Prussians.
The Poles began to threaten, and the Finns began to flap at him,
Directing all the blame for this unfortunate mishap at him;
While the Swedes withdrew entirely from the Anglo-Saxon dailies
The right of photographing the Aurora Borealis,
And, all efforts at rapprochement in the meantime proving barren,
The Japanese in self-defence annexed the Isle of Arran.
My platypus, once thought to be more cautious and more tentative
Than any other living diplomatic representative,
Was now a sort of warning to all diplomatic students
Of the risks attached to negligence, the perils of imprudence,
And, branded in the Honours List as 'Platypus, Dame Vera,'
Retired, a lonely figure, to lay eggs at Bordighera.

EDGAR BATEMAN 1860–1946

IT'S A GREAT BIG SHAME

I've lost a pal, 'e's the best in all the tahn,
But don't you fink 'im dead, becos 'e aint –
But since 'e's wed 'e 'as 'ad ter knuckle dahn –
It's enuf to wex the temper of a saint!
'E's a brewer's drayman wiv a leg o' mutton fist,
An' as strong as a bullick or an 'orse –
Yet in 'er 'ands 'e's like a little kid –
Oh! I wish as I could get 'im a divorce.

Chorus:
It's a great big shame, an' if she belonged ter me
I'd let 'er know who's who –
Naggin' at a feller wot is six foot free,
And 'er only four foot two!
Oh! they 'adn't been married not a month nor more,
When underneath her fumb goes Jim –
Oh, isn't it a pity as the likes of 'er
Should put upon the likes of 'im?

Now Jim was class 'e could sing a decent song,
And at scrappin' 'e 'ad won some great renown;
It took two coppers for ter make 'im move along,
And annuvver six to 'old the feller dahn.
But today when I axes would 'e come an' 'ave some beer,
To the doorstep on tip-toe 'e arrives;
'I daresn't,' says 'e 'Don't shout, cos she'll 'ear
I've got ter clean the windows an' the knives.'

33

On a Sunday morn, wiv a dozen pals or more,
'E'd play at pitch and toss along the Lea;
But now she bullies 'im a scrubbin' 'o the floor
Such a change, well, I never did see.
Wiv a apron on 'im, I twigged 'im, on 'is knees
A rubbin' up the old 'arf stone;
Wot wiv emptyin' the ashes and a-shellin' o' the peas,
I'm blowed if 'e can call 'is self 'is own!

Chorus:
It's a great big shame, etc.

SIR MAX BEERBOHM 1872–1956

from OLD SURREY SAWS AND SAYINGS

Collected and communicated by Sir Max Beerbohm, PRA
(Professor of Rural Archaeology)

A red sky at night
Is a shepherd's delight,
A red sky in the morning
Is a shepherd's warning,
A sky that looks bad
Is a shepherd's plaid,
A good-looking sky
Is a shepherd's pie.

HILAIRE BELLOC 1870–1953

MATILDA
WHO TOLD LIES, AND WAS BURNED TO DEATH

Matilda told such Dreadful Lies,
It made one Gasp and Stretch one's Eyes;
Her Aunt, who, from her Earliest Youth,
Had kept a Strict Regard for Truth,
Attempted to Believe Matilda:
The effort very nearly killed her,
And would have done so, had not She
Discovered this Infirmity.
For once, towards the Close of Day,
Matilda, growing tired of play,
And finding she was left alone,
Went tiptoe to the Telephone
And summoned the Immediate Aid
Of London's Noble Fire-Brigade.
Within an hour the Gallant Band
Were pouring in on every hand,
From Putney, Hackney Downs, and Bow
With Courage high and Hearts a-glow
They galloped, roaring through the Town,
'Matilda's House is Burning Down!'
Inspired by British Cheers and Loud
Proceeding from the Frenzied Crowd,
They ran their ladders through a score
Of windows on the Ball Room Floor;
And took Peculiar Pains to Souse
The Pictures up and down the House,
Until Matilda's Aunt succeeded
In showing them they were not needed;
And even then she had to pay
To get the Men to go away!

• • •

It happened that a few Weeks later
Her Aunt was off to the Theatre
To see that Interesting Play
The Second Mrs Tanqueray.
She had refused to take her Niece
To hear this Entertaining Piece:
A Deprivation Just and Wise
To Punish her for Telling Lies.
That Night a Fire *did* break out –
You should have heard Matilda Shout!
You should have heard her Scream and Bawl,
And throw the window up and call
To People passing in the Street –
(The rapidly increasing Heat
Encouraging her to obtain
Their confidence) – but all in vain!
For every time She shouted 'Fire!'
They only answered 'Little Liar!'
And therefore when her Aunt returned,
Matilda, and the House, were Burned.

HILAIRE BELLOC 1870–1953

REBECCA
WHO SLAMMED DOORS FOR FUN
AND PERISHED MISERABLY

A Trick that everyone abhors
In Little Girls is slamming Doors,
A Wealthy Banker's Little Daughter
Who lived in Palace Green, Bayswater
(By name Rebecca Offendort),
Was given to this Furious Sport.

She would deliberately go
And Slam the door like Billy-Ho!
To make her Uncle Jacob start.
She was not really bad at heart,
But only rather rude and wild:
She was an aggravating child . . .

It happened that a Marble Bust
Of Abraham was standing just
Above the Door this little lamb
Had carefully prepared to Slam,
And Down it came! It knocked her flat!
It laid her out! She looked like that.

• • •

Her funeral Sermon (which was long
And followed by a Sacred Song)
Mentioned her Virtues, it is true,
But dwelt upon her Vices too,
And showed the Dreadful End of One
Who goes and slams the door for Fun.

• • •

The children who were brought to hear
The awful Tale from far and near
Were much impressed, and inly swore
They never more would slam the Door.
– As often they had done before.

HILAIRE BELLOC 1870–1953

HENRY KING
WHO CHEWED BITS OF STRING, AND WAS EARLY
CUT OFF IN DREADFUL AGONIES

The Chief Defect of Henry King
    Was chewing little bits of String.
At last he swallowed some which tied
    Itself in ugly Knots inside.
Physicians of the Utmost Fame
Were called at once; but when they came
They answered, as they took their Fees,
'There is no Cure for this Disease.
Henry will very soon be dead.'
His Parents stood about his Bed
Lamenting his Untimely Death,
When Henry, with his Latest Breath,
Cried – 'Oh, my Friends, be warned by me,
That Breakfast, Dinner, Lunch, and Tea
Are all the Human Frame requires . . . '
With that, the Wretched Child expires.

HILAIRE BELLOC 1870–1953

LORD FINCHLEY

Lord Finchley tried to mend the Electric Light
Himself. It struck him dead: And serve him right!
It is the business of the wealthy man
To give employment to the artisan.

HILAIRE BELLOC 1870–1953

THE FROG

Be kind and tender to the Frog,
    And do not call him names,
As 'Slimy skin', or 'Polly-wog',
    Or likewise 'Ugly James',
Or 'Gap-a-grin', or 'Toad-gone-wrong',
    Or 'Billy Bandy-knees':
The Frog is justly sensitive
    To epithets like these.
No animal will more repay
    A treatment kind and fair;
At least so lonely people say
    Who keep a frog (and, by the way,
They are extremely rare).

E. C. BENTLEY 1875–1956

CLERIHEWS

(i)

Wynkyn de Worde
Had as funny a name as ever I heard.
Of what could they have been thinking
When they called him Wynkyn?

(ii)

It only irritated Brahms
To tickle him under the arms.
What really helped him to compose
Was to be stroked on the nose.

(iii)

When their lordships asked Bacon
How many bribes he had taken
He had at least the grace
To get very red in the face.

(iv)

Mr. Henry Ford
Had a little secret hoard,
To which he would add a dime
From time to time.

(v)

George the Third
Ought never to have occurred.
One can only wonder
At so grotesque a blunder.

(vi)

There exists no proof as
To who shot William Rufus,
But shooting him would seem
To have been quite a sound scheme.

(vii)

'Susaddah!' exclaimed Ibsen,
'By dose is turdig cribson!
I'd better dot kiss you,
Atishoo! Atishoo!'

(viii)

'Dinner-time?' said Gilbert White,
'Yes, yes – certainly – all right.
Just let me finish this note
About the Lesser White-bellied Stoat.'

SIR JOHN BETJEMAN 1906–84

HOW TO GET ON IN SOCIETY

Phone for the fish-knives, Norman
    As Cook is a little unnerved;
You kiddies have crumpled the serviettes
    And I must have things daintily served.

Are the requisites all in the toilet?
    The frills round the cutlets can wait
Till the girl has replenished the cruets
    And switched on the logs in the grate.

It's ever so close in the lounge dear,
    But the vestibule's comfy for tea
And Howard is out riding on horseback
    So do come and take some with me.

Now here is a fork for your pastries
    And do use the couch for your feet;
I know what I wanted to ask you –
    Is trifle sufficient for sweet?

Milk and then just as it comes dear?
    I'm afraid the preserve's full of stones;
Beg pardon, I'm soiling the doileys
    With afternoon tea-cakes and scones.

SIR JOHN BETJEMAN 1906–84

A SUBALTERN'S LOVE-SONG

Miss J. Hunter Dunn, Miss J. Hunter Dunn,
Furnish'd and burnish'd by Aldershot sun,
What strenuous singles we played after tea,
We in the tournament – you against me!

Love-thirty, love-forty, oh! weakness of joy,
The speed of a swallow, the grace of a boy,
With carefullest carelessness, gaily you won,
I am weak from your loveliness, Joan Hunter Dunn.

Miss Joan Hunter Dunn, Miss Joan Hunter Dunn,
How mad I am, sad I am, glad that you won.
The warm-handled racket is back in its press,
But my shock-headed victor, she loves me no less.

Her father's euonymus shines as we walk,
And swing past the summer-house, buried in talk,
And cool the verandah that welcomes us in
To the six-o'clock news and a lime-juice and gin.

The scent of the conifers, sound of the bath,
The view from my bedroom of moss-dappled path,
As I struggle with double-end evening tie,
For we dance at the Golf Club, my victor and I.

On the floor of her bedroom lie blazer and shorts
And the cream-coloured walls are be-trophied with sports,
And westering, questioning settles the sun
On your low-leaded window, Miss Joan Hunter Dunn.

The Hillman is waiting, the light's in the hall,
The pictures of Egypt are bright on the wall,
My sweet, I am standing beside the oak stair
And there on the landing's the light on your hair.

By roads 'not adopted,' by woodlanded ways,
She drove to the club in the late summer haze,
Into nine-o'clock Camberley, heavy with bells
And mushroomy, pine-woody, evergreen smells.

Miss Joan Hunter Dunn, Miss Joan Hunter Dunn,
I can hear from the car-park the dance has begun.
Oh! full Surrey twilight! importunate band!
Oh! strongly adorable tennis-girl's hand!

Around us are Rovers and Austins afar,
Above us, the intimate roof of the car,
And here on my right is the girl of my choice,
With the tilt of her nose and the chime of her voice,

And the scent of her wrap, and the words never said,
And the ominous, ominous dancing ahead.
We sat in the car park till twenty to one
And now I'm engaged to Miss Joan Hunter Dunn.

SIR JOHN BETJEMAN 1906–84

HUNTER TRIALS

It's awf'lly bad luck on Diana,
    Her ponies have swallowed their bits;
She fished down their throats with a spanner
    And frightened them all into fits.

So now she's attempting to borrow.
    Do lend her some bits, Mummy, *do*;
I'll lend her my own for to-morrow,
    But to-day *I*'ll be wanting them too.

Just look at Prunella on Guzzle,
    The wizardest pony on earth;
Why doesn't she slacken his muzzle
    And tighten the breech in his girth?

I say, Mummy, there's Mrs Geyser
    And doesn't she look pretty sick?
I bet it's because Mona Lisa
    Was hit on the hock with a brick.

Miss Blewitt says Monica threw it,
    But Monica says it was Joan,
And Joan's very thick with Miss Blewitt,
    So Monica's sulking alone.

And Margaret failed in her paces,
    Her withers got tied in a noose,
So her coronets caught in the traces
    And now all her fetlocks are loose.

Oh, it's me now. I'm terribly nervous.
    I wonder if Smudges will shy.
She's practically certain to swerve as
    Her Pelham is over one eye.

* * *

Oh wasn't it naughty of Smudges?
    Oh, Mummy, I'm sick with disgust.
She threw me in front of the Judges,
    And my silly old collarbone's bust.

CAPTAIN HAMISH BLAIR

THE BLOODY ORKNEYS

This bloody town's a bloody cuss –
No bloody trains, no bloody bus,
And no one cares for bloody us –
    In bloody Orkney.

The bloody roads are bloody bad,
The bloody folks are bloody mad,
They'd make the brightest bloody sad,
    In bloody Orkney.

All bloody clouds, and bloody rains,
No bloody kerbs, no bloody drains,
The Council's got no bloody brains,
    In bloody Orkney.

Everything's so bloody dear,
A bloody bob, for bloody beer,
And is it good? – no bloody fear,
    In bloody Orkney.

The bloody 'flicks' are bloody old,
The bloody seats are bloody cold,
You can't get in for bloody gold
    In bloody Orkney.

The bloody dances make you smile,
The bloody band is bloody vile,
It only cramps your bloody style,
    In bloody Orkney.

No bloody sport, no bloody games,
No bloody fun, the bloody dames
Won't even give their bloody names
    In bloody Orkney.

Best bloody place is bloody bed,
With bloody ice on bloody head,
You might as well be bloody dead,
    In bloody Orkney.

GARY BOSWELL 1960–

DUCKS DON'T SHOP IN SAINSBURYS

You can't get millet at Sainsburys
and they don't sell grass or weed
it's a total dead loss
for heather and moss
and they don't stock sunflower seed.

They've got some fish in the freezer
but they're low on rats and mice
and you're out of luck
if you're a debonair duck
and you want to buy something nice

'cos none of their bread is stale
and they've stopped selling hay and straw.
Let's face it, if you were a duck in Sainsburys,
you'd be heading for the exit door!

TOM BROWN 1663–1704

DOCTOR FELL

I do not love thee, Doctor Fell.
The reason why, I cannot tell;
But this I know, and know full well,
I do not love thee, Doctor Fell.

GELETT BURGESS 1866–1951

THE PURPLE COW

I never saw a Purple Cow,
I never hope to see one;
But I can tell you, anyhow,
I'd rather see than be one.

LEWIS CARROLL 1832–98

FATHER WILLIAM

'You are old, Father William,' the young man said,
'And your hair has become very white;
And yet you incessantly stand on your head –
Do you think, at your age, it is right?'

'In my youth,' Father William replied to his son,
'I feared it might injure the brain;
But, now that I'm perfectly sure I have none,
Why, I do it again and again.'

'You are old,' said the youth, 'as I mentioned before,
And have grown most uncommonly fat;
Yet you turned a back-somersault in at the door –
Pray, what is the reason of that?'

'In my youth,' said the sage, as he shook his grey locks,
'I kept all my limbs very supple
By the use of this ointment – one shilling the box –
Allow me to sell you a couple?'

'You are old,' said the youth, 'and your jaws are too weak
For anything tougher than suet;
Yet you finished the goose, with the bones and the beak –
Pray, how did you manage to do it?'

'In my youth,' said his father, 'I took to the law,
And argued each case with my wife;
And the muscular strength, which it gave to my jaw,
Has lasted the rest of my life.'

'You are old,' said the youth, 'one would hardly suppose
    That your eye was as steady as ever;
Yet you balanced an eel on the end of your nose –
    What made you so awfully clever?'

'I have answered three questions, and that is enough,'
    Said his father; 'don't give yourself airs!
Do you think I can listen all day to such stuff?
    Be off, or I'll kick you down stairs!'

LEWIS CARROLL 1832–98

THE WALRUS AND THE CARPENTER

The sun was shining on the sea,
   Shining with all his might:
He did his very best to make
   The billows smooth and bright –
And this was odd, because it was
   The middle of the night.

The moon was shining sulkily,
   Because she thought the sun
Had got no business to be there
   After the day was done –
'It's very rude of him,' she said,
   'To come and spoil the fun!'

The sea was wet as wet could be,
   The sands were dry as dry.
You could not see a cloud, because
   No cloud was in the sky:
No birds were flying overhead –
   There were no birds to fly.

The Walrus and the Carpenter
   Were walking close at hand:
They wept like anything to see
   Such quantities of sand:
'If this were only cleared away,'
   They said, 'it *would* be grand!'

'If seven maids with seven mops
   Swept it for half a year,
Do you suppose,' the Walrus said,
   'That they could get it clear?'
'I doubt it,' said the Carpenter,
   And shed a bitter tear.

'O Oysters, come and walk with us!'
    The Walrus did beseech.
'A pleasant walk, a pleasant talk,
    Along the briny beach:
We cannot do with more than four,
    To give a hand to each.'

The eldest Oyster looked at him,
    But not a word he said:
The eldest Oyster winked his eye,
    And shook his heavy head –
Meaning to say he did not choose
    To leave the oyster-bed.

But four young Oysters hurried up,
    All eager for the treat:
Their coats were brushed, their faces washed
    Their shoes were clean and neat –
And this was odd, because, you know,
    They hadn't any feet.

Four other Oysters followed them,
    And yet another four;
And thick and fast they came at last,
    And more, and more, and more –
All hopping through the frothy waves,
    And scrambling to the shore.

The Walrus and the Carpenter
    Walked on a mile or so,
And then they rested on a rock
    Conveniently low:
And all the little Oysters stood
    And waited in a row.

'The time has come,' the Walrus said,
  'To talk of many things:
Of shoes – and ships – and sealing wax –
  Of cabbages – and kings –
And why the sea is boiling hot –
  And whether pigs have wings.'

'But wait a bit,' the Oysters cried,
  'Before we have our chat;
For some of us are out of breath,
  And all of us are fat!'
'No hurry!' said the Carpenter.
  They thanked him much for that.

'A loaf of bread,' the Walrus said,
  'Is what we chiefly need:
Pepper and vinegar besides
  Are very good indeed –
Now, if you're ready, Oysters dear,
  We can begin to feed.'

'But not on us!' the Oysters cried,
  Turning a little blue.
'After such kindness that would be
  A dismal thing to do!'
'The night is fine,' the Walrus said,
  'Do you admire the view?

'It was so kind of you to come,
    And you are very nice!'
The Carpenter said nothing but
    'Cut us another slice.
I wish you were not quite so deaf –
    I've had to ask you twice!'

'It seems a shame,' the Walrus said,
    'To play them such a trick.
After we've brought them out so far,
    And made them trot so quick!'
The Carpenter said nothing but
    'The butter's spread too thick!'

'I weep for you,' the Walrus said:
    'I deeply sympathize.'
With sobs and tears he sorted out
    Those of the largest size,
Holding his pocket-handkerchief
    Before his streaming eyes.

'O Oysters,' said the Carpenter,
    'You've had a pleasant run!
Shall we be trotting home again?'
    But answer came there none –
And this was scarcely odd, because
    They'd eaten every one.

LEWIS CARROLL 1832–98

JABBERWOCKY

'Twas brillig, and the slithy toves
  Did gyre and gimble in the wabe;
All mimsy were the borogoves,
    And the mome raths outgrabe.

'Beware the Jabberwock, my son!
  The jaws that bite, the claws that catch!
Beware the Jubjub bird and shun
    The frumious Bandersnatch!'

He took his vorpal sword in hand:
  Long time the manxome foe he sought –
So rested he by the Tumtum tree,
    And stood awhile in thought.

And as in uffish thought he stood,
  The Jabberwock, with eyes of flame,
Came whiffling through the tulgey wood,
    And burbled as it came!

One, two! One, two! And through and through
  The vorpal blade went snicker-snack!
He left it dead, and with its head
    He went galumphing back.

'And hast thou slain the Jabberwock!
  Come to my arms, my beamish boy!
O frabjous day! Callooh! Callay!'
    He chortled in his joy.

'Twas brillig, and the slithy toves
  Did gyre and gimble in the wabe;
All mimsy were the borogoves,
    And the mome raths outgrabe.

LEWIS CARROLL 1832–98

SPEAK ROUGHLY TO YOUR LITTLE BOY

Speak roughly to your little boy,
   And beat him when he sneezes;
He only does it to annoy,
   Because he knows it teases.
        Chorus: WOW! WOW! WOW!

I speak severely to my boy,
   I beat him when he sneezes;
For he can thoroughly enjoy
   The pepper when he pleases!
        Chorus: WOW! WOW! WOW!

LEWIS CARROLL 1832–98

from THE HUNTING OF THE SNARK
FIT THE FIRST
The Landing

'Just the place for a Snark!' the Bellman cried,
    As he landed his crew with care;
Supporting each man on the top of the tide
    By a finger entwined in his hair.

'Just the place for a Snark! I have said it twice:
    That alone should encourage the crew.
Just the place for a Snark! I have said it thrice:
    What I tell you three times is true.'

The crew was complete: it included a Boots –
    A maker of Bonnets and Hoods –
A Barrister, brought to arrange their disputes –
    And a Broker, to value their goods.

A Billiard-marker, whose skill was immense,
    Might perhaps have won more than his share –
But a Banker, engaged at enormous expense,
    Had the whole of their cash in his care.

There was also a Beaver, that paced on the deck,
    Or would sit making lace in the bow:
And had often (the Bellman said) saved them from wreck,
    Though none of the sailors knew how.

There was one who was famed for the number of things
    He forgot when he entered the ship:
His umbrella, his watch, all his jewels and rings,
    And the clothes he had bought for the trip.

He had forty-two boxes, all carefully packed,
    With his name painted clearly on each:
But, since he omitted to mention the fact,
    They were all left behind on the beach.

The loss of his clothes hardly mattered, because
    He had seven coats on when he came,
With three pairs of boots – but the worst of it was,
    He had wholly forgotten his name.

He would answer to 'Hi!' or to any loud cry,
    Such as 'Fry me!' or 'Fritter my wig!'
To 'What-you-may-call-um!' or 'What-was-his-name!'
    But especially 'Thing-um-a-jig!'

While, for those who preferred a more forcible word,
    He had different names from these:
His intimate friends called him 'Candle-ends,'
    And his enemies 'Toasted-cheese.'

'His form is ungainly – his intellect small – '
    (So the Bellman would often remark)
'But his courage is perfect! And that, after all,
    Is the thing that one needs with a Snark.'

He would joke with hyaenas, returning their stare
    With an impudent wag of the head:
And he once went a walk, paw-in-paw, with a bear,
    'Just to keep up its spirits,' he said.

He came as a Baker: but owned when too late –
    And it drove the poor Bellman half-mad –
He could only bake Bridecake – for which, I may state,
    No materials were to be had.

The last of the crew needs especial remark,
    Though he looked an incredible dunce:
He had just one idea – but, that one being 'Snark',
    The good Bellman engaged him at once.

He came as a Butcher: but gravely declared,
    When the ship had been sailing a week,
He could only kill Beavers. The Bellman looked scared,
    And was almost too frightened to speak:

But at length he explained, in a tremulous tone,
    There was only one Beaver on board;
And that was a tame one he had of his own,
    Whose death would be deeply deplored.

The Beaver, who happened to hear the remark,
    Protested, with tears in its eyes,
That not even the rapture of hunting the Snark
    Could atone for that dismal surprise!

It strongly advised that the Butcher should be
    Conveyed in a separate ship:
But the Bellman declared that would never agree
    With the plans he had made for the trip:

Navigation was always a difficult art,
    Though with only one ship and one bell:
And he feared he must really decline, for his part,
    Undertaking another as well.

The Beaver's best course was, no doubt, to procure
    A second-hand dagger-proof coat –
So the Baker advised it – and next, to insure
    Its life in some Office of note:

This the Banker suggested, and offered for hire
    (On moderate terms), or for sale,
Two excellent Policies, one Against Fire,
    And one Against Damage from Hail.

Yet still, ever after that sorrowful day,
    Whenever the Butcher was by,
The Beaver kept looking the opposite way,
    And appeared unaccountably shy.

WENDY COPE 1945–

BLOODY MEN

Bloody men are like bloody buses –
You wait for about a year
And as soon as one approaches your stop
Two or three others appear.

You look at them flashing their indicators,
Offering you a ride.
You're trying to read the destinations,
You haven't much time to decide.

If you make a mistake, there is no turning back.
Jump off, and you'll stand there and gaze
While the cars and the taxis and lorries go by
And the minutes, the hours, the days.

WENDY COPE 1945–

LONELY HEARTS

Can someone make my simple wish come true?
Male biker seeks female for touring fun.
Do you live in North London? Is it you?

Gay vegetarian whose friends are few,
I'm into music, Shakespeare and the sun.
Can someone make my simple wish come true?

Executive in search of something new –
Perhaps bisexual woman, arty, young.
Do you live in North London? Is it you?

Successful, straight and solvent? I am too –
Attractive Jewish lady with a son.
Can someone make my simple wish come true?

I'm Libran, inexperienced and blue –
Need slim non-smoker, under twenty-one.
Do you live in North London? Is it you?

Please write (with photo) to Box 152
Who knows where it may lead once we've begun?
Can someone make my simple wish come true?
Do you live in North London? Is it you?

E. E. CUMMINGS 1884–1962

NOBODY LOSES ALL THE TIME

nobody loses all the time

i had an uncle named
Sol who was a born failure and
nearly everybody said he should have gone
into vaudeville perhaps because my Uncle Sol could
sing McCann He Was A Diver on Xmas Eve like Hell Itself which
may or may not account for the fact that my Uncle

Sol indulged in that possibly most inexcusable
of all to use a highfalootin phrase
luxuries that is or to
wit farming and be
it needlessly
added

my Uncle Sol's farm
failed because the chickens
ate the vegetables so
my Uncle Sol had a
chicken farm till the
skunks ate the chickens when

my Uncle Sol
had a skunk farm but
the skunks caught cold and
died and so
my Uncle Sol imitated the
skunks in a subtle manner

or by drowning himself in the watertank
but somebody who'd given my Uncle Sol a Victor
Victrola and records while he lived presented to
him upon the auspicious occasion of his decease a
scrumptious not to mention splendiferous funeral with
tall boys in black gloves and flowers and everything and

i remember we all cried like the Missouri
when my Uncle Sol's coffin lurched because
somebody pressed a button
(and down went
my Uncle
Sol

and started a worm farm)

E. E. CUMMINGS 1894–1962

MAY I FEEL SAID HE

may i feel said he
(i'll squeal said she
just once said he)
it's fun said she

(may i touch said he
how much said she
a lot said he)
why not said she

(let's go said he
not too far said she
what's too far said he
where you are said she)

may i stay said he
(which way said she
like this said he
if you kiss said she

may i move said he
is it love said she)
if you're willing said he
(but you're killing said she

but it's life said he
but your wife said she
now said he)
ow said she

(tiptop said he
don't stop said she
oh no said he)
go slow said she

(cccome?said he
ummm said she)
you're divine!said he
(you are Mine said she)

ROALD DAHL 1916–90

ST IVES

As I was going to St Ives
I met a man with seven wives.
Said he, 'I think it's much more fun
Than getting stuck with only one.'

ROALD DAHL 1916–90

HOT AND COLD

A woman who my mother knows
Came in and took off all her clothes.

Said I, not being very old,
'By golly gosh, you must be cold!'

'No, no!' she cried. 'Indeed I'm not!
I'm feeling devilishly hot!'

ROALD DAHL 1916–90

LITTLE RED RIDING HOOD AND THE WOLF

As soon as Wolf began to feel
That he would like a decent meal,
He went and knocked on Grandma's door.
When Grandma opened it, she saw
The sharp white teeth, the horrid grin,
And Wolfie said, 'May I come in?'
Poor Grandmamma was terrified,
'He's going to eat me up!' she cried.
And she was absolutely right.
He ate her up in one big bite.
But Grandmamma was small and tough,
And Wolfie wailed, 'That's not enough!
'I haven't yet begun to feel
'That I have had a decent meal!'
He ran around the kitchen yelping,
'I've *got* to have another helping!'
Then added with a frightful leer,
'I'm therefore going to wait right here
'Till Little Miss Red Riding Hood
'Comes home from walking in the wood.'
He quickly put on Grandma's clothes,
(Of course he hadn't eaten those.)
He dressed himself in coat and hat.
He put on shoes and after that
He even brushed and curled his hair,
Then sat himself in Grandma's chair.
In came the little girl in red.
She stopped. She stared. And then she said,

'*What great big ears you have, Grandma.*'
'*All the better to hear you with,*' the Wolf replied.
'*What great big eyes you have, Grandma,*'
     said Little Red Riding Hood.
'*All the better to see you with,*' the Wolf replied.

He sat there watching her and smiled.
He thought, I'm going to eat this child.
Compared with her old Grandmamma
She's going to taste like caviare.

Then Little Red Riding Hood said, '*But Grandma,
what a lovely great big furry coat you have on.*'

'That's wrong!' cried Wolf. 'Have you forgot
'To tell me what BIG TEETH I've got?
'Ah well, no matter what you say,
'I'm going to eat you anyway.'
The small girl smiles. One eyelid flickers.
She whips a pistol from her knickers.
She aims it at the creature's head
And *bang bang bang*, she shoots him dead.
A few weeks later, in the wood,
I came across Miss Riding Hood.
But what a change! No cloak of red,
No silly hood upon her head.
She said, 'Hello, and do please note
'My lovely furry WOLFSKIN COAT.'

ROALD DAHL 1916–90

A HAND IN THE BIRD

I am a maiden who is forty,
And a maiden I shall stay.
There are some who call me haughty,
But I care not what they say.

I was running the tombola
At our church bazaar today,
And doing it with gusto
In my usual jolly way . . .

When suddenly, I knew not why,
There came a funny feeling
Of something *crawling up my thigh*!
I nearly hit the ceiling!

A mouse! I thought. How foul! How mean!
How exquisitely tickly!
Quite soon I know I'm going to scream.
I've got to catch it quickly.

I made a grab. I caught the mouse,
Now right inside my knickers.
A mouse my foot! It was a HAND!
Great Scott! It was the vicar's!

PAUL DEHN 1912–76

ALTERNATIVE ENDINGS TO AN UNWRITTEN BALLAD

I stole through the dungeons, while everyone slept,
  Till I came to the cage where the Monster was kept.
There, locked in the arms of a Giant Baboon,
  Rigid and smiling, lay . . . MRS RAVOON!

I climbed the clock-tower in the first morning sun
  And 'twas midday at least ere my journey was done;
But the clock never sounded the last stroke of noon,
  For there, from the clapper, swung MRS RAVOON.

I hauled in the line, and I took my first look
  At the half-eaten horror that hung from the hook.
I had dragged from the depths of the limpid lagoon
  The luminous body of MRS RAVOON.

I fled in the storm, through lightning and thunder,
  And there, as a flash split the darkness asunder,
Chewing a rat's-tail and mumbling a rune,
  Mad in the moat squatted MRS RAVOON.

I stood by the waters so green and so thick,
  And I stirred at the scum with my old, withered stick;
When there rose through the ooze, like a monstrous balloon,
  The bloated cadaver of MRS RAVOON.

Facing the fens, I looked back from the shore
  Where all had been empty a moment before;
And there, by the light of the Lincolnshire moon,
  Immense on the marshes, stood . . . MRS RAVOON!

JOHN DONNE 1572–1631

SONG

Go, and catch a falling star,
  Get with child a mandrake root,
Tell me, where all past years are,
  Or who cleft the Devil's foot,
Teach me to hear mermaids singing,
  Or to keep off envy's stinging,
      And find
      What wind
Serves to advance an honest mind.

If thou be'est born to strange sights,
  Things invisible to see,
Ride ten thousand days and nights,
  Till age snow white hairs on thee,
Thou, when thou return'st, wilt tell me
All strange wonders that befell thee,
      And swear
      No where
Lives a woman true, and fair.

If thou find'st one, let me know,
  Such a pilgrimage were sweet,
Yet do not, I would not go,
  Though at next door we might meet,
Though she were true, when you met her,
And last, till you write your letter,
      Yet she
      Will be
False, ere I come, to two, or three.

PAUL DURCAN 1944–

TULLYNOE: TÊTE-À-TÊTE IN THE PARISH PRIEST'S PARLOUR

"Ah, he was a grand man."
"He was: he fell out of the train going to Sligo."
"He did: he thought he was going to the lavatory."
"He did: in fact he stepped out the rear door of the train."
"He did: God, he must have got an awful fright."
"He did: he saw that it wasn't the lavatory at all."
"He did: he saw that it was the railway tracks going away from him."
"He did: I wonder if . . . but he was a grand man."
"He was: he had the most expensive Toyota you can buy."
"He had: well, it was only beautiful."
"It was: he used to have an Audi."
"He had: as a matter of fact he used to have two Audis."
"He had: and then he had an Avenger."
"He had: and then he had a Volvo."
"He had: in the beginning he had a lot of Volkses."
"He had: he was a great man for the Volkses."
"He was: did he once have an Escort?"
"He had not: he had a son a doctor."
"He had: and he had a Morris Minor too."
"He had: he had a sister a hairdresser in Killmallock."
"He had: he had another sister a hairdresser in Ballybunnion."
"He had: he was put in a coffin which was put in his father's cart."
"He was: his lady wife sat on top of the coffin driving the donkey."
"She did: Ah, but he was a grand man."
"He was: he was a grand man . . . "
"Goodnight, Father."
"Goodnight, Mary."

MARRIOTT EDGAR 1880–1951

THE LION AND ALBERT

There's a famous seaside place called Blackpool,
    That's noted for fresh air and fun,
And Mr and Mrs Ramsbottom
    Went there with young Albert, their son.

A grand little lad was young Albert,
    All dressed in his best; quite a swell
With a stick with an 'orse's 'ead 'andle,
    The finest that Woolworth's could sell.

They didn't think much to the Ocean:
    The waves, they was fiddlin' and small,
There was no wrecks and nobody drownded,
    Fact, nothing to laugh at at all.

So, seeking for further amusement,
    They paid and went into the Zoo,
Where they'd Lions and Tigers and Camels,
    And old ale and sandwiches too.

There were one great big Lion called Wallace;
    His nose were all covered with scars –
He lay in a somnolent posture,
    With the side of his face on the bars.

Now Albert had heard about Lions,
    How they was ferocious and wild –
To see Wallace lying so peaceful,
    Well, it didn't seem right to the child.

So straightway the brave little feller,
    Not showing a morsel of fear,
Took his stick with its 'orse's 'ead 'andle
    And pushed it in Wallace's ear.

You could see that the Lion didn't like it,
    For giving a kind of a roll,
He pulled Albert inside the cage with 'im,
    And swallowed the little lad 'ole.

Then Pa, who had seen the occurrence,
    And didn't know what to do next,
Said 'Mother! Yon Lion's 'et Albert',
    And Mother said 'Well, I am vexed!'

Then Mr and Mrs Ramsbottom –
    Quite rightly, when all's said and done –
Complained to the Animal Keeper,
    That the Lion had eaten their son.

The keeper was quite nice about it;
    He said 'What a nasty mishap.
Are you sure that it's *your* boy he's eaten?'
    Pa said 'Am I sure? There's his cap!'

The manager had to be sent for.
    He came and he said 'What's to do?'
Pa said 'Yon Lion's 'et Albert,
    And 'im in his Sunday clothes, too.'

Then Mother said, 'Right's right, young feller;
    I think it's a shame and a sin,
For a lion to go and eat Albert,
    And after we've paid to come in.'

The manager wanted no trouble,
    He took out his purse right away,
Saying 'How much to settle the matter?'
    And Pa said 'What do you usually pay?'

But Mother had turned a bit awkward
    When she thought where her Albert had gone.
She said 'No! someone's got to be summonsed' –
    So that was decided upon.

Then off they went to the P'lice Station,
    In front of the Magistrate chap;
They told 'im what happened to Albert,
    And proved it by showing his cap.

The Magistrate gave his opinion
    That no one was really to blame
And he said that he hoped the Ramsbottoms
    Would have further sons to their name.

At that Mother got proper blazing,
    'And thank you, sir, kindly,' said she.
'What waste all our lives raising children
    To feed ruddy Lions? Not me!'

T. S. ELIOT 1888–1965

BUSTOPHER JONES: THE CAT ABOUT TOWN

Bustopher Jones is *not* skin and bones –
In fact, he's remarkably fat.
He doesn't haunt pubs – he has eight or nine clubs,
For he's the St James's Street Cat!
He's the cat we all greet as he walks down the street
In his coat of fastidious black:
No commonplace mousers have such well-cut trousers
Or such an impeccable back.
In the whole of St James's the smartest of names is
The name of this Brummell of Cats;
And we're all of us proud to be nodded or bowed to
By Bustopher Jones in white spats!

His visits are occasional to the *Senior Educational*
And it is against the rules
For any one Cat to belong both to that
And the *Joint Superior Schools*.
For a similar reason, when game is in season
He is found, not at *Fox's*, but *Blimp's*;
But he's frequently seen at the gay *Stage and Screen*
Which is famous for winkles and shrimps.
In the season of venison he gives his ben'son
To the *Pothunter's* succulent bones;
And just before noon's not a moment too soon
To drop in for a drink at the *Drones*.
When he's seen in a hurry there's probably curry
At the *Siamese* – or at the *Glutton*;
If he looks full of gloom then he's lunched at the *Tomb*
On cabbage, rice pudding and mutton.

So, much in this way, passes Bustopher's day –
At one club or another he's found.
It can be no surprise that under our eyes
He has grown unmistakably round.
He's a twenty-five pounder, or I am a bounder,
And he's putting on weight every day:
But he's so well preserved because he's observed
All his life a routine, so he'd say.
Or, to put it in rhyme: 'I shall last out my time'
Is the word for this stoutest of Cats.
It must and it shall be Spring in Pall Mall
While Bustopher Jones wears white spats!

T. S. ELIOT 1888–1965

MACAVITY: THE MYSTERY CAT

Macavity's a Mystery Cat: he's called the Hidden Paw –
For he's the master criminal who can defy the Law.
He's the bafflement of Scotland Yard, the Flying Squad's despair:
For when they reach the scene of crime – *Macavity's not there!*

Macavity, Macavity, there's no one like Macavity,
He's broken every human law, he breaks the law of gravity.
His powers of levitation would make a fakir stare,
And when you reach the scene of crime – *Macavity's not there!*
You may seek him in the basement, you may look up in the air –
But I tell you once and once again, *Macavity's not there!*

Macavity's a ginger cat, he's very tall and thin;
You would know him if you saw him, for his eyes are sunken in.
His brow is deeply lined with thought, his head is highly domed;
His coat is dusty from neglect, his whiskers are uncombed.
He sways his head from side to side, with movements like a snake;
And when you think he's half asleep, he's always wide awake.

Macavity, Macavity, there's no one like Macavity,
For he's a fiend in feline shape, a monster of depravity.
You may meet him in a by-street, you may see him in the square –
But when a crime's discovered, then *Macavity's not there!*

He's outwardly respectable. (They say he cheats at cards.)
And his footprints are not found in any file of Scotland Yard's.
And when the larder's looted, or the jewel-case is rifled,
Or when the milk is missing, or another Peke's been stifled,
Or the greenhouse glass is broken, and the trellis past repair –
Ay, there's the wonder of the thing! *Macavity's not there!*

And when the Foreign Office find a Treaty's gone astray,
Or the Admiralty lose some plans and drawings by the way,
There may be a scrap of paper in the hall or on the stair –
But it's useless to investigate – *Macavity's not there!*
And when the loss has been disclosed, the Secret Service say:
'It *must* have been Macavity!' – but he's a mile away.
You'll be sure to find him resting, or a-licking of his thumbs,
Or engaged in doing complicated long division sums.

Macavity, Macavity, there's no one like Macavity,
There never was a Cat of such deceitfulness and suavity.
He always has an alibi, and one or two to spare:
At whatever time the deed took place – MACAVITY WASN'T THERE!
And they say that all the Cats whose wicked deeds are widely known,
(I might mention Mungojerrie, I might mention Griddlebone)
Are nothing more than agents for the Cat who all the time
Just controls their operations: the Napoleon of Crime.

GAVIN EWART 1916–95

THE BLACK BOX

As well as these poor poems
I am writing some wonderful ones.
They are all being filed separately,
nobody sees them.

When I die they will be buried
in a big black tin box.
In fifty years' time
they must be dug up,

for so my will provides.
This is to confound the critics
and teach everybody
a valuable lesson.

MICHAEL FLANDERS 1922–75

THE HIPPOPOTAMUS SONG

A bold Hippopotamus was standing one day
On the banks of the cool Shalimar.
He gazed at the bottom as it peacefully lay
By the light of the evening star.
Away on a hilltop sat combing her hair
His fair Hippopotamine maid;
The Hippopotamus was no ignoramus
And sang her this sweet serenade.

> Mud, Mud, glorious mud,
> Nothing quite like it for cooling the blood!
> So follow me, follow
> Down to the hollow
> And there let us wallow
> In glorious mud!

The fair Hippopotama he aimed to entice
From her seat on that hilltop above,
As she hadn't got a ma to give her advice,
Came tiptoeing down to her love.
Like thunder the forest re-echoed the sound
Of the song that they sang as they met.
His inamorata adjusted her garter
And lifted her voice in duet.

> Mud, Mud, glorious mud,
> Nothing quite like it for cooling the blood!
> So follow me, follow,
> Down to the hollow
> And there let us wallow
> In glorious mud!

Now more Hippopotami began to convene
On the banks of that river so wide.
I wonder now what am I to say of the scene
That ensued by the Shalimar side?
They dived all at once with an ear-splitting splosh
Then rose to the surface again,
A regular army of Hippopotami
All singing this haunting refrain.

Mud! Mud! Glorious mud!
Nothing quite like it for cooling the blood.
So follow me, follow,
Down to the hollow
And there let us wallow
In glorious mud!

W. S. GILBERT 1836–1911

THE NIGHTMARE

When you're lying awake with a dismal headache, and repose is taboo'd
     by anxiety,
I conceive you may use any language you choose to indulge in, without
     impropriety;
For your brain is on fire – the bedclothes conspire of usual slumber to
     plunder you:
First your counterpane goes, and uncovers your toes, and your sheet
     slips demurely from under you;
Then the blanketing tickles – you feel like mixed pickles – so terribly
     sharp is the pricking,
And you're hot, and you're cross, and you tumble and toss till there's
     nothing 'twixt you and the ticking.
Then the bedclothes all creep to the ground in a heap, and you pick 'em
     all up in a tangle;
Next your pillow resigns and politely declines to remain at its usual
     angle!
Well, you get some repose in the form of a doze, with hot eye-balls and
     head ever aching,
But your slumbering teems with such horrible dreams that you'd very
     much better be waking;
For you dream you are crossing the Channel, and tossing about in a
     steamer from Harwich –
Which is something between a large bathing machine and a very small
     second-class carriage –
And you're giving a treat (penny ice and cold meat) to a party of friends
     and relations –
They're a ravenous horde – and they all came on board at Sloane Square
     and South Kensington Stations.
And bound on that journey you find your attorney (who started that
     morning from Devon);

He's a bit undersized, and you don't feel surprised when he tells you
    he's only eleven.
Well, you're driving like mad with this singular lad (by-the-bye the
    ship's now a four-wheeler),
And you're playing round games, and he calls you bad names when you
    tell him that 'ties pay the dealer';
But this you can't stand, so you throw up your hand, and you find
    you're as cold as an icicle,
In your shirt and your socks (the black silk with gold clocks), crossing
    Salisbury Plain on a bicycle:
And he and the crew are on bicycles too – which they've somehow or
    other invested in –
And he's telling the tars, all the particu*lars* of a company he's
    interested in –
It's a scheme of devices, to get at low prices, all goods from cough
    mixtures to cables
(Which tickled the sailors) by treating retailers, as though they were
    all vege*ta*bles –
You get a good spadesman to plant a small tradesman, (first take off his
    boots with a boot-tree),
And his legs will take root, and his fingers will shoot, and they'll
    blossom and bud like a fruit-tree –
From the greengrocer tree you get grapes and green pea, cauliflower,
    pineapple, and cranberries,
While the pastrycook plant, cherry brandy will grant, apple puffs, and
    three-corners, and banberries –
The shares are a penny, and ever so many are taken by Rothschild and
    Baring,
And just as a few are allotted to you, you awake with a shudder
    despairing –

You're a regular wreck, with a crick in your neck, and no wonder you
snore, for your head's on the floor, and you've needles and pins
from your soles to your shins, and your flesh is a-creep for your
left leg's asleep, and you've cramp in your toes, and a fly on your
nose, and some fluff in your lung, and a feverish tongue, and a
thirst that's intense, and a general sense that you haven't been
sleeping in clover;
But the darkness has passed, and it's daylight at last, and the night has
been long – ditto ditto my song – and thank goodness they're
both of them over!

HARRY GRAHAM 1874–1936

L'ENFANT GLACÉ

When Baby's cries grew hard to bear
I popped him in the Frigidaire.
I never would have done so if
I'd known that he'd be frozen stiff.
My wife said: 'George, I'm so unhappé!
Our darling's now completely *frappé*!'

HARRY GRAHAM 1874–1936

OPPORTUNITY

When Mrs Gorm (Aunt Eloise)
Was stung to death by savage bees,
Her husband (Prebendary Gorm)
Put on his veil, and took the swarm.
He's publishing a book next May
On 'How to Make Bee-keeping Pay'.

JOYCE GRENFELL 1910–79

STATELY AS A GALLEON

My neighbour, Mrs Fanshaw, is portly-plump and gay,
She must be over sixty-seven, if she is a day.
You might have thought her life was dull,
It's one long whirl instead.
I asked her all about it, and this is what she said:

I've joined an Olde Thyme Dance Club, the trouble is that there
Are too many ladies over, and no gentlemen to spare.
It seems a shame, it's not the same,
But still it has to be,
Some ladies have to dance together,
One of them is me.

Stately as a galleon, I sail across the floor,
Doing the Military Two-step, as in the days of yore.
I dance with Mrs Tiverton; she's light on her feet, in spite
Of turning the scale at fourteen stone, and being of medium height.
So gay the band,
So giddy the sight,
Full evening dress is a must,
But the zest goes out of a beautiful waltz
When you dance it bust to bust.

So, stately as two galleons, we sail across the floor,
Doing the Valse Valeta as in the days of yore.
The gent is Mrs Tiverton, I am her lady fair,
She bows to me ever so nicely and I curtsey to her with care.
So gay the band,
So giddy the sight,
But it's not the same in the end
For a lady is never a gentleman, though
She may be your bosom friend.

So, stately as a galleon, I sail across the floor,
Doing the dear old Lancers, as in the days of yore.
I'm led by Mrs Tiverton, she swings me round and round
And though she manoeuvres me wonderfully well
I never get off the ground.
So gay the band,
So giddy the sight,
I try not to get depressed.
And it's done me a power of good to explode,
And get this lot off my chest.

JOHN HEGLEY 1953–

MALCOLM

Miserable Malcolm from Morcambe
had Rottweilers but would not walk 'em.
They were stuck in all day
but no muck would they lay
because Malcambe had managed to cork 'em.

JOHN HEGLEY 1953–

IN THE ARMS OF MY GLASSES

they can call me softy
as ofty
as they please
but still I'll stand by these
my little optical accessories
they stop me walking into lampposts
and trees
when it's foggy
and I'm out walking with my doggie

JOHN HEGLEY 1953–

A COMPARISON OF LOGS AND DOGS

both are very popular at Christmas
but it is not generally considered cruel
to abandon a log
and dogs are rarely used as fuel

STANLEY HOLLOWAY 1890–1982

OLD SAM

It occurred on the evening before Waterloo
And troops were lined up on Parade,
And Sergeant inspecting 'em, he was a terror
Of whom every man was afraid –

All excepting one man who was in the front rank,
A man by the name of Sam Small,
And 'im and the Sergeant were both 'daggers drawn',
They thought 'nowt' of each other at all.

As Sergeant walked past he was swinging his arm,
And he happened to brush against Sam,
And knocking his musket clean out of his hand
It fell to the ground with a slam.

'Pick it oop,' said Sergeant, abrupt like but cool,
But Sam with a shake of his head
Said 'Seeing as tha' knocked it out of me hand,
P'raps tha'll pick the thing oop instead.'

'Sam, Sam, pick oop tha' musket,'
The Sergeant exclaimed with a roar.
Sam said 'Tha' knocked it doon, Reet!
Then tha'll pick it oop, or it stays where it is, on't floor.'

The sound of high words
Very soon reached the ears of an Officer, Lieutenant Bird,
Who says to the Sergeant, 'Now what's all this 'ere?'
And the Sergeant told what had occurred.

'Sam, Sam, pick oop tha' musket,'
Lieutenant exclaimed with some heat.
Sam said 'He knocked it doon, Reet! then he'll pick it oop,
Or it stays where it is, at me feet.'

It caused quite a stir when the Captain arrived
To find out the cause of the trouble;
And every man there, all excepting Old Sam,
Was full of excitement and bubble.

'Sam, Sam, pick oop tha' musket,'
Said Captain for strictness renowned.
Sam said 'He knocked it doon, Reet!
Then he'll pick it oop, or it stays where it is on't ground.'

The same thing occurred when the Major and Colonel
Both tried to get Sam to see sense,
But when Old Duke o' Wellington came into view
Well, the excitement was tense.

Up rode the Duke on a lovely white 'orse,
To find out the cause of the bother;
He looks at the musket and then at Old Sam
And he talked to Old Sam like a brother,

'Sam, Sam, pick oop tha' musket,'
The Duke said as quiet as could be,
'Sam, Sam, pick oop tha' musket
Coom on, lad, just to please me.'

'Alright, Duke,' said Old Sam, 'just for thee I'll oblige,
And to show thee I meant no offence.'
So Sam picked it up, 'Gradeley, lad,' said the Duke,
'Right-o, boys, let battle commence.'

A. E. HOUSMAN 1859–1936

THE SHADES OF NIGHT

The shades of night were falling fast,
    And the rain was falling faster,
When through an Alpine village passed
    An Alpine village pastor:
A youth who bore mid snow and ice
    A bird that wouldn't chirrup,
And a banner with the strange device –
    'Mrs Winslow's soothing syrup.'

'Beware the pass,' the old man said,
    'My bold, my desperate fellah;
Dark lowers the tempest overhead,
    And you'll want your umberella;
And the roaring torrent is deep and wide –
    You may hear how loud it washes.'
But still that clarion voice replied:
    'I've got my old goloshes.'

'Oh, stay,' the maiden said, 'and rest
    (For the wind blows from the nor'ward)
Thy weary head upon my breast –
    And please don't think I'm forward.'
A tear stood in his bright blue eye,
    And he gladly would have tarried;
But still he answered with a sigh:
    'Unhappily I'm married.'

LEIGH HUNT 1784–1859

TO A FISH

You strange, astonished-looking, angle-faced,
    Dreary-mouthed, gaping wretches of the sea,
    Gulping salt-water everlastingly,
Cold-blooded, though with red your blood be graced,
And mute, though dwellers in the roaring waste;
    And you, all shapes beside, that fishy be, –
    Some round, some flat, some long, all devilry,
Legless, unloving, infamously chaste; –

O scaly, slippery, wet, swift, staring wights,
    What is't ye do? What life lead? eh, dull goggles?
How do ye vary your vile days and nights?
    How pass your Sundays? Are ye still but joggles
In ceaseless wash? Still nought but gapes, and bites,
    And drinks, and stares, diversified with boggles?

A FISH ANSWERS

Amazing monster! that, for aught I know,
    With the first sight of thee didst make our race
    For ever stare! O flat and shocking face,
Grimly divided from the breast below!
Thou that on dry land horribly dost go
    With a split body and most ridiculous pace,
    Prong after prong, disgracer of all grace,
Long-useless-finned, haired, upright, unwet, slow!

O breather of unbreathable, sword-sharp air,
    How canst exist? How bear thyself, thou dry
And dreary sloth? What particle canst share
    Of the only blessed life, the watery?
I sometimes see of ye an actual *pair*
    Go by! linked fin by fin! most odiously.

CHRISTOPHER ISHERWOOD 1904–86

THE COMMON CORMORANT

The common cormorant (or shag)
Lays eggs inside a paper bag,
You follow the idea, no doubt?
It's to keep the lightning out.

But what these unobservant birds
Have never thought of, is that herds
Of wandering bears might come with buns
And steal the bags to hold the crumbs.

CLIVE JAMES 1939–

THE BOOK OF MY ENEMY HAS BEEN REMAINDERED

The book of my enemy has been remaindered
And I am pleased.
In vast quantities it has been remaindered.
Like a van-load of counterfeit that has been seized
And sits in piles in a police warehouse,
My enemy's much-prized effort sits in piles
In the kind of bookshop where remaindering occurs.
Great, square stacks of rejected books and, between them, aisles
One passes down reflecting on life's vanities,
Pausing to remember all those thoughtful reviews
Lavished to no avail upon one's enemy's book –
For behold, here is that book
Among these ranks and banks of duds,
These ponderous and seemingly irreducible cairns
Of complete stiffs.

The book of my enemy has been remaindered
And I rejoice.
It has gone with bowed head like a defeated legion
Beneath the yoke.
What avail him now his awards and prizes,
The praise expended upon his meticulous technique,
His individual new voice?
Knocked into the middle of next week
His brainchild now consorts with the bad buys,
The sinkers, clinkers, dogs and dregs,
The Edsels of the world of movable type,
The bummers that no amount of hype could shift,
The unbudgeable turkeys.

Yea, his slim volume with its understated wrapper
Bathes in the glare of the brightly jacketed *Hitler's War Machine*,
His unmistakably individual new voice
Shares the same scrapyard with a forlorn skyscraper
Of *The Kung-Fu Cookbook*,
His honesty, proclaimed by himself and believed in by others,
His renowned abhorrence of all posturing and pretence,
Is there with *Pertwee's Promenades and Pierrots –*
One Hundred Years of Seaside Entertainment,
And (oh, this above all) his sensibility,
His sensibility and its hair-like filaments,
His delicate, quivering sensibility is now as one
With *Barbara Windsor's Book of Boobs*,
A volume graced by the descriptive rubric
'My boobs will give everyone hours of fun.'

Soon now a book of mine could be remaindered also,
Though not to the monumental extent
In which the chastisement of remaindering has been meted out
To the book of my enemy,
Since in the case of my own book it will be due
To a miscalculated print run, a marketing error –
Nothing to do with merit.
But just supposing that such an event should hold
Some slight element of sadness, it will be offset
By the memory of this sweet moment.
Chill the champagne and polish the crystal goblets!
The book of my enemy has been remaindered
And I am glad.

JENNY JOSEPH 1932–

WARNING

When I am an old woman I shall wear purple
With a red hat which doesn't go, and doesn't suit me,
And I shall spend my pension on brandy and summer gloves
And satin sandals, and say we've no money for butter.
I shall sit down on the pavement when I'm tired
And gobble up samples in shops and press alarm bells
And run my stick along the public railings
And make up for the sobriety of my youth.
I shall go out in my slippers in the rain
And pick the flowers in other people's gardens
And learn to spit.

You can wear terrible shirts and grow more fat
And eat three pounds of sausages at a go
Or only bread and pickle for a week
And hoard pens and pencils and beermats and things in boxes.

But now we must have clothes that keep us dry
And pay our rent and not swear in the street
And set a good example for the children.
We must have friends to dinner and read the papers.

But maybe I ought to practise a little now?
So people who know me are not too shocked and surprised
When suddenly I am old, and start to wear purple.

JOHN KEATS 1795–1821

ALL THESE ARE VILE

The House of Mourning written by Mr Scott,
   A sermon at the Magdalen, a tear
   Dropped on a greasy novel, want of cheer
After a walk uphill to a friend's cot,
Tea with a maiden lady, a cursed lot
   Of worthy poems with the author near,
   A patron lord, a drunkenness from beer,
Haydon's great picture, a cold coffee pot
At midnight when the muse is ripe for labour,
   The voice of Mr Coleridge, a French bonnet
Before you in the pit, a pipe and tabour,
A damned inseparable flute and neighbour –
   All these are vile. But viler Wordsworth's sonnet
   On Dover. Dover! Who *could* write upon it?

Mr Scott is John Scott, first editor of the *London Magazine* which was established in 1820. The Magdalen refers to the Magdalen Hospital, a refuge for reformed prostitutes. Benjamin Haydon was famous for his historical and biblical paintings.

X. J. KENNEDY 1929–

TO SOMEONE WHO INSISTED I LOOK UP SOMEONE

I rang them up while touring Timbuctoo,
Those bosom chums to whom you're known as '*Who?*'

EDWARD LEAR 1812–88

THE OWL AND THE PUSSY-CAT

I

The Owl and the Pussy-cat went to sea
  In a beautiful pea-green boat,
They took some honey, and plenty of money,
  Wrapped up in a five-pound note.
The Owl looked up to the stars above,
  And sang to a small guitar,
'O lovely Pussy! O Pussy, my love,
  What a beautiful Pussy you are,
      You are,
      You are!
  What a beautiful Pussy you are!'

II

Pussy said to the Owl, 'You elegant fowl!
  How charmingly sweet you sing!
O let us be married! too long we have tarried:
  But what shall we do for a ring?'
They sailed away, for a year and a day,
  To the land where the Bong-tree grows
And there in a wood a Piggy-wig stood
  With a ring at the end of his nose,
      His nose,
      His nose,
  With a ring at the end of his nose.

III

'Dear Pig, are you willing to sell for one shilling
  Your ring?' Said the Piggy, 'I will.'
So they took it away, and were married next day
  By the Turkey who lives on the hill.
They dined on mince, and slices of quince,
  Which they ate with a runcible spoon;
And hand in hand, on the edge of the sand,
  They danced by the light of the moon,
      The moon,
      The moon,
  They danced by the light of the moon.

EDWARD LEAR 1812–88

THE COURTSHIP OF THE YONGHY-BONGHY-BÒ

I

On the Coast of Coromandel
    Where the early pumpkins blow,
        In the middle of the woods
        Lived the Yonghy-Bonghy-Bò.
Two old chairs, and half a candle, –
One old jug without a handle, –
        These were all his worldly goods:
        In the middle of the woods,
        These were all the worldly goods,
    Of the Yonghy-Bonghy-Bò,
    Of the Yonghy-Bonghy-Bò.

II

Once, among the Bong-trees walking
    Where the early pumpkins blow,
        To a little heap of stones
        Came the Yonghy-Bonghy-Bò.
There he heard a Lady talking,
To some milk-white Hens of Dorking, –
        ''Tis the Lady Jingly Jones!
        On that little heap of stones
        Sits the Lady Jingly Jones!'
    Said the Yonghy-Bonghy-Bò.
    Said the Yonghy-Bonghy-Bò.

III

'Lady Jingly! Lady Jingly!
    Sitting where the pumpkins blow,
        Will you come and be my wife?'
    Said the Yonghy-Bonghy-Bò.
'I am tired of living singly, –
On this coast so wild and shingly, –

I'm a-weary of my life;
   If you'll come and be my wife,
      Quite serene would be my life!' –
Said the Yonghy-Bonghy-Bò.
Said the Yonghy-Bonghy-Bò.

IV

'On this Coast of Coromandel,
   Shrimps and watercresses grow,
      Prawns are plentiful and cheap,'
Said the Yonghy-Bonghy-Bò.
'You shall have my chairs and candle,
And my jug without a handle! –
      Gaze upon the rolling deep
      (Fish is plentiful and cheap);
      As the sea, my love is deep!'
Said the Yonghy-Bonghy-Bò.
Said the Yonghy-Bonghy-Bò.

V

Lady Jingly answered sadly,
   And her tears began to flow, –
      'Your proposal comes too late,
Mr Yonghy-Bonghy-Bò!
I would be your wife most gladly!'
(Here she twirled her fingers madly)
      'But in England I've a mate!
      Yes! you've asked me far too late,
      For in England I've a mate,
Mr Yonghy-Bonghy-Bò!
Mr Yonghy-Bonghy-Bò.

VI

'Mr Jones – (his name is Handel, –
   Handel Jones, Esquire, & Co.)
      Dorking fowls delights to send,
   Mr Yonghy-Bonghy-Bò!
Keep, oh! keep your chairs and candle,
And your jug without a handle, –
      I can merely be your friend!
      – Should my Jones more Dorkings send,
      I will give you three, my friend!
   Mr Yonghy-Bonghy-Bò!
   Mr Yonghy-Bonghy-Bò!

VII

'Though you've such a tiny body,
   And your head so large doth grow, –
      Though your hat may blow away,
   Mr Yonghy-Bonghy-Bò!
Though you're such a Hoddy Doddy –
Yet I wish that I could modi-
      fy the words I needs must say!
      Will you please to go away?
      That is all I have to say –
   Mr Yonghy-Bonghy-Bò!
   Mr Yonghy-Bonghy-Bò!'

VIII

Down the slippery slopes of Myrtle,
   Where the early pumpkins blow,
      To the calm and silent sea
   Fled the Yonghy-Bonghy-Bò.
There, beyond the Bay of Gurtle,
Lay a large and lively Turtle: –
      'You're the Cove,' he said, 'for me;

On your back beyond the sea,
  Turtle, you shall carry me!'
Said the Yonghy-Bonghy-Bò,
Said the Yonghy-Bonghy-Bò.

IX

Through the silent-roaring ocean
  Did the Turtle swiftly go;
    Holding fast upon his shell
  Rode the Yonghy-Bonghy-Bò.
With a sad primaeval motion
Towards the sunset isles of Boshen
    Still the Turtle bore him well.
    Holding fast upon his shell,
    'Lady Jingly Jones, farewell!'
Sang the Yonghy-Bonghy-Bò,
Sang the Yonghy-Bonghy-Bò.

X

From the Coast of Coromandel,
  Did that Lady never go;
    On that heap of stones she mourns
  For the Yonghy-Bonghy-Bò.
On that Coast of Coromandel,
In his jug without a handle,
    Still she weeps, and daily moans,
    On that little heap of stones
    To her Dorking Hens she moans,
  For the Yonghy-Bonghy-Bò,
  For the Yonghy-Bonghy-Bò.

EDWARD LEAR 1812–88

LIMERICKS

(i)

There was an Old Man in a boat,
Who said, 'I'm afloat! I'm afloat!'
When they said, 'No! you ain't!' he was ready to faint,
That unhappy Old Man in a boat.

(ii)

There was a young person whose history,
Was always considered a mystery;
She sate in a ditch, although no one knew which,
And composed a small treatise on history.

(iii)

There was an Old Man of Toulouse
Who purchased a new pair of shoes;
When they asked, 'Are they pleasant?' – He said, 'Not at present!'
That turbid old man of Toulouse.

(iv)

There was a Young Lady of Portugal,
Whose ideas were excessively nautical:
She climbed up a tree, to examine the sea,
But declared she would never leave Portugal.

(v)

There was an Old Man with a beard,
Who said, 'It is just as I feared! –
    Two Owls and a Hen, four Larks and a Wren,
Have all built their nests in my beard!'

(vi)

There was an Old Man of Hong Kong,
Who never did anything wrong;
    He lay on his back, with his head in a sack,
That innocuous Old Man of Hong Kong.

EDWARD LEAR 1812–88

THE POBBLE WHO HAS NO TOES

I

The Pobble who has no toes
    Had once as many as we;
When they said, 'Some day you may lose them all'; –
    He replied, – 'Fish fiddle de-dee!'
And his Aunt Jobiska made him drink,
Lavender water tinged with pink,
For she said, 'The World in general knows
There's nothing so good for a Pobble's toes!'

II

The Pobble who has no toes,
    Swam across the Bristol Channel;
But before he set out he wrapped his nose,
    In a piece of scarlet flannel.
For his Aunt Jobiska said, 'No harm
'Can come to his toes if his nose is warm;
'And it's perfectly known that a Pobble's toes
'Are safe, – provided he minds his nose.'

III

The Pobble swam fast and well,
    And when boats or ships came near him
He tinkledy-binkledy-winkled a bell,
    So that all the world could hear him.
And all the Sailors and Admirals cried,
When they saw him nearing the further side, –
'He has gone to fish, for his Aunt Jobiska's
'Runcible Cat with crimson whiskers!'

IV

But before he touched the shore,
    The shore of the Bristol Channel,
A sea-green Porpoise carried away
    His wrapper of scarlet flannel.
And when he came to observe his feet,
Formerly garnished with toes so neat,
His face at once became forlorn
On perceiving that all his toes were gone!

V

And nobody ever knew
    From that dark day to the present,
Whoso had taken the Pobble's toes,
    In a manner so far from pleasant.
Whether the shrimps or crawfish gray,
Or crafty Mermaids stole them away –
Nobody knew; and nobody knows
How the Pobble was robbed of his twice five toes!

VI

The Pobble who has no toes
    Was placed in a friendly Bark,
And they rowed him back, and carried him up,
    To his Aunt Jobiska's Park.
And she made him a feast at his earnest wish
Of eggs and buttercups fried with fish; –
And she said, – 'It's a fact the whole world knows,
'That Pobbles are happier without their toes.'

EDWARD LEAR 1812–88

THE AKOND OF SWAT

Who or why, or which, or *what*,
                    Is the Akond of SWAT?

Is he tall or short, or dark or fair?
Does he sit on a stool or a sofa or chair,   or SQUAT,
                    The Akond of Swat?

Is he wise or foolish, young or old?
Does he drink his soup and his coffee cold,   or HOT,
                    The Akond of Swat?

Does he sing or whistle, jabber or talk,
And when riding abroad does he gallop or walk,   or TROT,
                    The Akond of Swat?

Does he wear a turban, a fez, or a hat?
Does he sleep on a mattress, a bed, or a mat,   or a COT,
                    The Akond of Swat?

When he writes a copy in round-hand size,
Does he cross his T's and finish his I's   with a DOT,
                    The Akond of Swat?

Can he write a letter concisely clear
Without a speck or a smudge or smear   or BLOT,
                    The Akond of Swat?

Do his people like him extremely well?
Or do they, whenever they can, rebel,   or PLOT,
                    At the Akond of Swat?

If he catches them then, either old or young,
Does he have them chopped in pieces or hung,   or SHOT,
                    The Akond of Swat?

Do his people prig in the lanes or park?
Or even at times, when days are dark,   GAROTTE?
                        O the Akond of Swat?

Does he study the wants of his own dominion?
Or doesn't he care for public opinion   a JOT,
                        The Akond of Swat?

To amuse his mind do his people show him
Pictures, or any one's last new poem,   or WHAT,
                        For the Akond of Swat?

At night if he suddenly screams and wakes,
Do they bring him only a few small cakes,   or a LOT,
                        For the Akond of Swat?

Does he live on turnips, tea, or tripe?
Does he like his shawl to be marked with a stripe,   or a DOT,
                        The Akond of Swat?

Does he like to lie on his back in a boat
Like the lady who lived in that isle remote,   SHALLOTT,
                        The Akond of Swat?

Is he quiet, or always making a fuss?
Is his steward a Swiss or a Swede or a Russ,   or a SCOT,
                        The Akond of Swat?

Does he like to sit by the calm blue wave?
Or to sleep and snore in a dark green cave,   or a GROT,
                        The Akond of Swat?

Does he drink small beer from a silver jug?
Or a bowl? or a glass? or a cup? or a mug?   or a POT,
                        The Akond of Swat?

Does he beat his wife with a gold-topped pipe,
When she lets the gooseberries grow too ripe,   or ROT,
                    The Akond of Swat?

Does he wear a white tie when he dines with friends,
And tie it neat in a bow with ends,   or a KNOT,
                    The Akond of Swat?

Does he like new cream, and hate mince-pies?
When he looks at the sun does he wink his eyes,   or NOT,
                    The Akond of Swat?

Does he teach his subjects to roast and bake?
Does he sail about on an inland lake,   in a YACHT,
                    The Akond of Swat?

Some one, or nobody, knows I wot
Who or which or why or what
                    Is the Akond of Swat!

ROGER McGOUGH 1937–

CAKE

i wanted one life
you wanted another
we couldn't have our cake
so we ate eachother.

ROGER McGOUGH 1937–

STINK

Sometimes I dont smell so good.
Its not that I dont care about
personal hygiene. I do. Its just that
sometimes the body catches up on me.
Like when Im out all day and
refuse to pay for a wash and
brush up at the local municipal
on lack of principle. And hiding
away in some unfamiliar un
kempt saloon I console myself
theres no such thing as *bad* breath.
All breath is good. And sweat
means the body functions as it
should. I drink my bitter.
Put a pork pie to the knife.
Far sweeter than the stink of
death, is the stink of life.

ROGER McGOUGH 1937–

SURVIVOR

Everyday,
I think about dying.
About disease, starvation,
violence, terrorism, war,
the end of the world.

It helps
keep my mind off things.

LOUIS MACNEICE 1907–63

BAGPIPE MUSIC

It's no go the merrygoround, it's no go the rickshaw,
All we want is a limousine and a ticket for the peepshow.
Their knickers are made of crêpe-de-chine,
    their shoes are made of python,
Their halls are lined with tiger rugs
    and their walls with heads of bison.

John MacDonald found a corpse, put it under the sofa,
Waited till it came to life and hit it with a poker,
Sold its eyes for souvenirs, sold its blood for whisky,
Kept its bones for dumb-bells to use when he was fifty.

It's no go the Yogi-Man, it's no go Blavatsky,
All we want is a bank balance and a bit of skirt in a taxi.

Annie MacDougall went to milk, caught her foot in the heather,
Woke to hear a dance record playing of Old Vienna.
It's no go your maidenheads, it's no go your culture,
All we want is a Dunlop tyre and the devil mend the puncture.

The Laird o' Phelps spent Hogmanay declaring he was sober,
Counted his feet to prove the fact and found he had one foot over.
Mrs. Carmichael had her fifth, looked at the job with repulsion,
Said to the midwife 'Take it away; I'm through with over-production'.

It's no go the gossip column, it's no go the Ceilidh,
All we want is a mother's help and a sugar-stick for the baby.

Willie Murray cut his thumb, couldn't count the damage,
Took the hide of an Ayrshire cow and used it for a bandage.
His brother caught three hundred cran when the seas were lavish,
Threw the bleeders back in the sea and went upon the parish.

It's no go the Herring Board, it's no go the Bible,
All we want is a packet of fags when our hands are idle.

It's no go the picture palace, it's no go the stadium,
It's no go the country cot with a pot of pink geraniums,
It's no go the Government grants, it's no go the elections,
Sit on your arse for fifty years and hang your hat on a pension.

It's no go my honey love, it's no go my poppet;
Work your hands from day to day, the winds will blow the profit.
The glass is falling hour by hour, the glass will fall for ever,
But if you break the bloody glass you won't hold up the weather.

SPIKE MILLIGAN 1918–

ON THE NING NANG NONG

On the Ning Nang Nong
Where the Cows go Bong!
And the Monkeys all say Boo!
There's a Nong Nang Ning
Where the trees go Ping!
And the tea pots Jibber Jabber Joo.
On the Nong Ning Nang
All the mice go Clang!
And you just can't catch 'em when they do!
So it's Ning Nang Nong!
Cows go Bong!
Nong Nang Ning!
Trees go Ping!
Nong Ning Nang!
The mice go Clang!
What a noisy place to belong,
Is the Ning Nang Ning Nang Nong!!

SPIKE MILLIGAN 1918–

FATHER THAMES

Let us look at the River Thames
One of England's watery gems,
Oily, brown, greasy, muddy,
Looking foul and smells of cruddy.
The Conservancy say they're cleaning it.
So why is it the colour of shit?

SPIKE MILLIGAN 1918–

BUMP!

Things that go 'bump' in the night
Should not really give one a fright.
It's the hole in each ear
That lets in the fear,
That, and the absence of light!

A. A. MILNE 1882–1956

THE KING'S BREAKFAST

The King asked
The Queen, and
The Queen asked
The Dairymaid:
'Could we have some butter for
The Royal slice of bread?'
The Queen asked
The Dairymaid,
The Dairymaid
Said: 'Certainly,
I'll go and tell
The cow
Now
Before she goes to bed.'

The Dairymaid
She curtsied,
And went and told
The Alderney:
'Don't forget the butter for
The Royal slice of bread.'
The Alderney
Said sleepily:
'You'd better tell
His Majesty
That many people nowadays
Like marmalade
Instead.'

The Dairymaid
Said: 'Fancy!'
And went to
Her Majesty.
She curtsied to the Queen, and
She turned a little red:

'Excuse me,
Your Majesty,
For taking of
The liberty,
But marmalade is tasty, if
It's very
Thickly
Spread.'

The Queen said:
'Oh!'
And went to
His Majesty:
'Talking of the butter for
The Royal slice of bread,
Many people
Think that
Marmalade
Is nicer.
Would you like to try a little
Marmalade
Instead?'

The King said:
'Bother!'
And then he said:
'Oh, deary me!'
The King sobbed: 'Oh, deary me!'
And went back to bed.
'Nobody,'
He whimpered,
'Could call me
A fussy man;
I *only* want
A little bit
Of butter for
My bread!'

The Queen said:
'There, there!'
And went to
The Dairymaid.
The Dairymaid
Said: 'There, there!'
And went to the shed.
The cow said:
'There, there!
I didn't really
Mean it;
Here's milk for his porringer
And butter for his bread.'

The Queen took
The butter
And brought it to
His Majesty;
The King said:
'Butter, eh?'
And bounced out of bed.
'Nobody,' he said:
As he kissed her
Tenderly,
'Nobody,' he said,
As he slid down
The banisters,
'Nobody,
My darling,
Could call me
A fussy man –
BUT
I do like a little bit of butter to my bread!'

ADRIAN MITCHELL 1932–

CELIA CELIA

When I am sad and weary
When I think all hope has gone
When I walk along High Holborn
I think of you with nothing on.

CHARLOTTE MITCHELL 1926–

JUST IN CASE

I'm going to the sea for the weekend,
in a couple of days I'll be back,
so I'll just take my little brown suit and a blouse
and a beret and carry my mac.

But what if the house is a cold one,
the house where I'm going to stay,
no fires after April, no hot drinks at night
and the windows wide open all day?
I'd better take one — no, *two* cardys
and my long tartan scarf for my head,
and my chaste new pyjamas in case they decide
to bring me my breakfast in bed.
And what about church on the Sunday?
I could wear my beret and suit,
but if it were sunny, it would be a chance
to wear my straw hat with the fruit.
I can't wear my little brown suit, though,
not with the straw with the fruit,
so I'll just take a silk dress to go with the straw
and a silk scarf to go with the suit.
I'll just take my jeans and that jumper
in case we go out in a car,
and my Guernsey in case we go out in a boat
and d'you know where my swimming things are?

D'you think I should take that black velvet
in case they've booked seats for a play?
And is it still usual to take your own towel
when you go somewhere to stay?
I had thought of just taking slippers,
but they do look disgustingly old,
I'd better take best shoes and sandals and boots
for the church and the heat and the cold.

I daren't go without my umbrella
in case I'm dressed up and it rains;
I'm bound to need socks and my wellies
for walking down long muddy lanes.

I'd rather not take my old dressing-gown,
it is such a business to pack,
but 'spose they have breakfast before they get dressed
I'd have to have mine in my mac.

I'm going to the sea for the weekend,
in a couple of days I'll be back,
so I'll just take my little brown suit and a blouse,
   two cardys, my long tartan scarf,
   my chaste new pyjamas,
   my straw hat with the fruit,
   my silk dress, my silk scarf,
   my jeans, that jumper,
   my Guernsey, my swimming things,
   my black velvet, my towel, my
   slippers (no one need see them)
   my sandals, my boots, my
   umbrella, my socks, my wellies,
   my dressing-gown, no, not
   my dressing-gown, OK my
   dressing-gown
and a beret and carry my mac.

THOMAS MOORE 1779–1852

ON TAKING A WIFE

'Come, come,' said Tom's father, 'at your time of life,
  There's no longer excuse for thus playing the rake.
It's time you should think, boy, of taking a wife.'
  'Why so it is, father. Whose wife shall I take?'

OGDEN NASH 1902–71

SONG OF THE OPEN ROAD

I think that I shall never see
A billboard lovely as a tree.
Indeed, unless the billboards fall
I'll never see a tree at all.

OGDEN NASH 1902–71

CURL UP AND DIET

Some ladies smoke too much and some ladies drink too much and
   some ladies pray too much,
But all ladies think that they weigh too much.
They may be as slender as a sylph or a dryad,
But just let them get on the scales and they embark on a doleful
   jeremiad:
No matter how low the figure the needle happens to touch,
They always claim it is at least five pounds too much;
To the world she may appear slinky and feline,
But she inspects herself in the mirror and cries, Oh, I look like a sea
   lion.
Yes, she tells you she is growing into the shape of a sea cow or manatee,
And if you say No, my dear, she says you are just lying to make her
   feel better, and if you say Yes, my dear, you injure her vanity.
Once upon a time there was a girl more beautiful and witty and
   charming than tongue can tell,
And she is now a dangerous raving maniac in a padded cell,
And the first indication her friends and relatives had that she was
   mentally overwrought
Was one day when she said, I weigh a hundred and twenty-seven,
   which is exactly what I ought.
Oh, often I am haunted
By the thought that somebody might someday discover a diet that
   would let ladies reduce just as much as they wanted,
Because I wonder if there is a woman in the world strong-minded
   enough to shed ten pounds or twenty,
And say There now, that's plenty;
And I fear me one ten-pound loss would only arouse the craving for
   another,
So it wouldn't do any good for ladies to get their ambition and look
   like somebody's fourteen-year-old brother,
Because, having accomplished this with ease,

They would next want to look like somebody's fourteen-year-old
    brother in the final stages of some obscure disease,
And the more success you have the more you want to get of it,
So then their goal would be to look like somebody's fourteen-year-old
    brother's ghost, or rather not the ghost itself, which is fairly solid,
    but a silhouette of it,
So I think it is very nice for ladies to be lithe and lissome.
But not so much so that you cut yourself if you happen to embrace
    or kissome.

DOROTHY PARKER 1893–1967

ONE PERFECT ROSE

A single flow'r he sent me, since we met.
All tenderly his messenger he chose;
Deep-hearted, pure, with scented dew still wet –
One perfect rose.

I knew the language of the floweret;
'My fragile leaves,' it said, 'his heart enclose.'
Love long has taken for his amulet
One perfect rose.

Why is it no one ever sent me yet
One perfect limousine, do you suppose?
Ah no, it's always just my luck to get
One perfect rose.

BRIAN PATTEN 1946–

HAIR TODAY, NO HER TOMORROW

'I've been upstairs,' she said.
'Oh yes?' I said.
'I found a hair,' she said.
'A hair?' I said.
'In the bed,' she said.
'From a head?' I said.
'It's not mine,' she said.
'Was it black?' I said.
'It was,' she said.
'I'll explain,' I said.
'You swine,' she said.
'Not quite,' I said.
'I'm going,' she said.
'Please don't,' I said.
'I hate you!' she said.
'You do?' I said.
'Of course,' she said.
'But why?' I said.
'That black hair,' she said.
'A pity,' I said.

'Time for truth,' she said.
'For confessions?' I said.
'Me too,' she said.
'You what?' I said.
'Someone else,' she said.
'Oh dear,' I said.
'So there!' she said.
'Ah well,' I said.
'Guess who?' she said.
'Don't say,' I said.
'I will,' she said.
'You would,' I said.
'Your friend,' she said.
'Oh damn,' I said.
'And his friend,' she said.

'Him too?' I said.
'And the rest,' she said.
'Good God,' I said.

'What's that?' she said.
'What's what?' I said.
'That noise?' she said.
'Upstairs?' I said.
'Yes,' she said.
'The new cat,' I said.
'A cat?' she said.
'It's black,' I said.
'Black?' she said.
'Long-haired,' I said.
'Oh no,' she said.
'Oh yes,' I said.
'Oh shit!' she said.
'Goodbye,' I said.

'I lied,' she said.
'You lied?' I said.
'Of course,' she said.
'About my friend?' I said.
'Y-ess,' she said.
'And the others?' I said.
'Ugh,' she said.
'How odd,' I said.
'I'm forgiven?' she said.
'Of course,' I said.
'I'll stay?' she said.
'Please don't,' I said.
'But why?' she said.
'I lied,' I said.
'About what?' she said.
'The new cat,' I said.
'It's white,' I said.

ALEXANDER POPE 1688–1744

EPIGRAM

engraved on the collar of a dog which I gave to his Royal
Highness Frederick Prince of Wales

I am his Highness' dog at Kew
Pray tell me, sir, whose dog are you?

SIR WALTER RALEIGH 1861–1922

WISHES OF AN ELDERLY MAN, WISHED AT A GARDEN PARTY, JUNE 1914

I wish I loved the Human Race;
I wish I loved its silly face;
I wish I loved the way it walks;
I wish I loved the way it talks;
And when I'm introduced to one
I wish I thought *What Jolly Fun!*

MICHAEL ROSEN 1946–

CHOCOLATE CAKE

I love chocolate cake.
And when I was a boy
I loved it even more.

Sometimes we used to have it for tea
and Mum used to say,
'If there's any left over
you can have it to take to school
tomorrow to have at playtime.'
And the next day I would take it to school
wrapped up in tin foil
open it up at playtime and sit in the
corner of the playground
eating it,
you know how the icing on top
is all shiny and it cracks as you
bite into it,
and there's that other kind of icing in
the middle
and it sticks to your hands and you
can lick your fingers
and lick your lips
oh it's lovely.
yeah.

Anyway,
once we had this chocolate cake for tea
and later I went to bed
but while I was in bed
I found myself waking up
licking my lips
and smiling.
I woke up proper.
'The chocolate cake.'
It was the first thing
I thought of.
I could almost see it
so I thought,
what if I go downstairs
and have a little nibble, yeah?

It was all dark
everyone was in bed
so it must have been really late
but I got out of bed,
crept out of the door

there's always a creaky floorboard, isn't there?

Past Mum and Dad's room,

careful not to tread on bits of broken toys
or bits of Lego
you know what it's like treading on Lego
with your bare feet,

yowwww
shhhhhhh

downstairs
into the kitchen
open the cupboard
and there it is
all shining.

So I take it out of the cupboard
put it on the table
and I see that
there's a few crumbs lying about on the plate,
so I lick my finger and run my finger all over the crumbs
scooping them up
and put them into my mouth.

ooooooommmmmmmmm

nice.

Then
I look again
and on one side where it's been cut,
it's all crumbly.

So I take a knife
I think I'll just tidy that up a bit,

cut off the crumbly bits
scoop them all up
and into the mouth

oooooommm mmmm
nice.

Look at the cake again.

That looks a bit funny now,
one side doesn't match the other
I'll just even it up a bit, eh?

Take the knife
and slice.
This time the knife makes a little cracky noise
as it goes through that hard icing on top.

A whole slice this time,

into the mouth.

Oh the icing on top
and the icing in the middle
ohhhhhh oooo mmmmmm.

But now
I can't stop myself
Knife –
I just take any old slice at it
and I've got this great big chunk
and I'm cramming it in
what a greedy pig
but it's so nice,

and there's another
and another and I'm squealing and I'm smacking my lips
and I'm stuffing myself with it
and
before I know
I've eaten the lot.
The whole lot.

I look at the plate.
It's all gone.

Oh no
they're bound to notice, aren't they,
a whole chocolate cake doesn't just disappear
does it?

What shall I do?

I know. I'll wash the plate up,
and the knife

and put them away and maybe no one
will notice, eh?

So I do that
and creep creep creep
back to bed
into bed
doze off
licking my lips
with a lovely feeling in my belly.
Mmmmmmmmmmm.

In the morning I get up,
downstairs,
have breakfast,
Mum's saying,
'Have you got your dinner money?'
and I say,
'Yes.'
'And don't forget to take some chocolate cake with you.'
I stopped breathing.

'What's the matter,' she says,
'you normally jump at chocolate cake?'

I'm still not breathing,
and she's looking at me very closely now.

She's looking at me just below my mouth.
'What's that?' she says.
'What's what?' I say.

145

'What's that there?'
'Where?'
'There,' she says, pointing at my chin.
'I don't know,' I say.
'It looks like chocolate,' she says.
'It's not chocolate is it?'
No answer.
'Is it?'
'I don't know.'
She goes to the cupboard
looks in, up, top, middle, bottom,
turns back to me.
'It's gone.
It's gone.
You haven't eaten it, have you?'
'I don't know.'
'You don't know. You don't know if you've eaten a whole
chocolate cake or not?
When? When did you eat it?'

So I told her,

and she said
well what could she say?
'That's the last time I give you any cake to take
to school.

Now go. Get out
no wait
not before you've washed your dirty sticky face.'
I went upstairs
looked in the mirror
and there it was,
just below my mouth,
a chocolate smudge.
The give-away.
Maybe she'll forget about it by next week.

ROBERT W. SERVICE 1874–1958
_____

THE CREMATION OF SAM McGEE

There are strange things done in the midnight sun
   By the men who moil for gold;
The Arctic trails have their secret tales
   That would make your blood run cold;
The Northern Lights have seen queer sights,
   But the queerest they ever did see
Was that night on the marge of Lake Lebarge
   I cremated Sam McGee.

Now Sam McGee was from Tennessee, where the cotton blooms and
   blows.
Why he left his home in the South to roam 'round the Pole, God only
   knows.
He was always cold, but the land of gold seemed to hold him like a
   spell;
Though he'd often say in his homely way that 'he'd sooner live in hell.'

On a Christmas Day we were mushing our way over the Dawson trail.
Talk of your cold! through the parka's fold it stabbed like a driven nail.
If our eyes we'd close, then the lashes froze till sometimes we couldn't
   see;
It wasn't much fun, but the only one to whimper was Sam McGee.

And that very night, as we lay packed tight in our robes beneath the
   snow,
And the dogs were fed, and the stars o'erhead were dancing heel and
   toe,
He turned to me, and 'Cap', says he, 'I'll cash in this trip, I guess;
And if I do, I'm asking that you won't refuse my last request.'

Well, he seemed so low that I couldn't say no; then he says with a sort
   of moan:
'It's the cursed cold, and it's got right hold till I'm chilled clean through
   to the bone.
Yet t'ain't being dead – it's my awful dread of the icy grave that pains;
So I want you to swear that, foul or fair, you'll cremate my last
   remains.'

A pal's last need is a thing to heed, so I swore I would not fail;
And we started on at the streak of dawn; but God! he looked ghastly
pale.
He crouched on the sleigh, and he raved all day of his home in
Tennessee;
And before nightfall a corpse was all that was left of Sam McGee.

There wasn't a breath in that land of death, and I hurried, horror-
driven,
With a corpse half hid that I couldn't get rid, because of a promise
given;
It was lashed to the sleigh, and it seemed to say: 'You may tax your
brawn and brains,
But you promised true, and it's up to you to cremate those last
remains.'

Now a promise made is a debt unpaid, and the trail has its own stern
code.
In the days to come, though my lips were dumb, in my heart how I
cursed that load.
In the long, long night, by the lone firelight, while the huskies, round in
a ring,
Howled out their woes to the homeless snows – O God! how I loathed
the thing.

And every day that quiet clay seemed to heavy and heavier grow;
And on I went, though the dogs were spent and the grub was getting
low;
The trail was bad, and I felt half mad, but I swore I would not give in;
And I'd often sing to the hateful thing, and it hearkened with a grin.

Till I came to the marge of Lake Lebarge, and a derelict there lay;
It was jammed in the ice, but I saw in a trice it was called the 'Alice
May'.
And I looked at it, and I thought a bit, and I looked at my frozen
chum;
Then 'Here', said I, with a sudden cry, 'is my cre-ma-tor-eum.'

Some planks I tore from the cabin floor, and I lit the boiler fire;
Some coal I found that was lying around, and I heaped the fuel higher;
The flames just soared, and the furnace roared – such a blaze you
    seldom see;
And I burrowed a hole in the glowing coal, and I stuffed in Sam
    McGee.

Then I made a hike, for I didn't like to hear him sizzle so;
And the heavens scowled, and the huskies howled, and the wind began
    to blow.
It was icy cold, but the hot sweat rolled down my cheeks, and I don't
    know why;
And the greasy smoke in an inky cloak went streaking down the sky.

I do not know how long in the snow I wrestled with grisly fear;
But the stars came out and they danced about ere again I ventured near;
I was sick with dread, but I bravely said: 'I'll just take a peep inside.
I guess he's cooked, and it's time I looked'; . . . then the door I opened
    wide.

And there sat Sam, looking cool and calm, in the heart of the furnace
    roar;
And he wore a smile you could see a mile, and he said: 'Please close that
    door.
It's fine in here, but I greatly fear you'll let in the cold and storm –
Since I left Plumtree, down in Tennessee, it's the first time I've been
    warm.'

> *There are strange things done in the midnight sun*
>   *By the men who moil for gold;*
> *The Arctic trails have their secret tales*
>   *That would make your blood run cold;*
> *The Northern Lights have seen queer sights,*
>   *But the queerest they ever did see*
> *Was that night on the marge of Lake Lebarge*
>   *I cremated Sam McGee.*

WILLIAM SHAKESPEARE 1564–1616

MY MISTRESS' EYES ARE NOTHING LIKE THE SUN

My mistress' eyes are nothing like the sun:
Coral is far more red than her lips' red:
If snow be white, why then her breasts are dun:
If hairs be wires, black wires grow on her head.
I have seen roses damask'd, red and white,
But no such roses see I in her cheeks:
And in some perfumes is there more delight
Than in the breath that from my mistress reeks.
I love to hear her speak, yet well I know
That music hath a far more pleasing sound:
I grant I never saw a goddess go, –
My mistress, when she walks, treads on the ground:
    And yet, by heaven, I think my love as rare
    As any she belied with false compare.

WILLIAM SHAKESPEARE 1564–1616

A SEA SONG
from *The Tempest*

The master, the swabber, the boatswain and I,
    The gunner and his mate,
Loved Mall, Meg, and Marian and Margery,
    But none of us cared for Kate;
    For she had a tongue with a tang,
    Would cry to a sailor, 'Go hang!'
She loved not the savour of tar nor of pitch,
Yet a tailor might scratch her where'er she did itch:
    Then to sea, boys, and let her go hang.

THOMAS SHERIDAN 1687–1738

A TRUE AND FAITHFUL INVENTORY
OF THE GOODS *BELONGING* TO DR. SWIFT,
VICAR OF LARA COR:
upon lending his House to the Bishop of Meath,
until his own was built

An Oaken, broken, Elbow-Chair;
A Cawdle-Cup, without an Ear;
A batter'd, shatter'd Ash Bedstead;
A Box of Deal, without a Lid;
A Pair of Tongs, but out of Joint;
A Back-Sword Poker, without Point;
A Pot that's crack'd across, around,
With an old knotted Garter bound;
An iron lock, without a Key;
A Wig, with hanging, quite grown grey;
A Curtain worn to Half a Stripe;
A Pair of Bellows, without Pipe;
A Dish, which might good Meat afford once;
An *Ovid*, and an old *Concordance*;
A Bottle Bottom, Wooden Platter,
One is for Meal, and one for Water;
There likewise is a Copper Skillet,
Which runs as fast out as you fill it;
A Candlestick, Snuff dish, and Save-all,
And thus his Household Goods you have all.
These, to your Lordship, as a Friend,
Till you have built, I freely lend;
They'll save your Lordship for a Shift;
Why not, as well as Doctor *Swift*?

SYDNEY SMITH 1771–1845

RECIPE FOR A SALAD

To make this condiment, your poet begs
The pounded yellow of two hard-boiled eggs;
Two boiled potatoes, passed through kitchen-sieve,
Smoothness and softness to the salad give;
Let onion atoms lurk within the bowl,
And, half-suspected, animate the whole.
Of mordant mustard add a single spoon,
Distrust the condiment that bites so soon;
But deem it not, thou man of herbs, a fault,
To add a double quantity of salt.
And, lastly, o'er the flavored compound toss
A magic soup-spoon of anchovy sauce.
Oh, green and glorious! Oh, herbaceous treat!
'T would tempt the dying anchorite to eat;
Back to the world he'd turn his fleeting soul,
And plunge his fingers in the salad bowl!
Serenely full, the epicure would say,
Fate can not harm me, I have dined to-day!

ERNEST LAWRENCE THAYER 1863–1940

CASEY AT THE BAT

The outlook wasn't brilliant for the Mudville nine that day;
The score stood four to two with but one inning more to play.
So when Cooney died at second, and Burrows did the same,
A pallor wreathed the features of the patrons of the game.
A straggling few got up to go in deep despair. The rest
Clung to the hope which springs eternal in the human breast;
They thought, 'If only Casey could but get a whack at that –
We'd put up even money now with Casey at the bat.'
But Flynn preceded Casey, as did also Jimmy Blake,
And the former was a lulu and the latter was a fake;
So upon that stricken multitude a deathlike silence sat,
For there seemed but little chance of Casey's getting to the bat.
But Flynn let drive a single, to the wonderment of all,
And Blake, the much despis-ed, tore the cover off the ball;
And when the dust had lifted, and the men saw what had occurred,
There was Jimmy safe at second and Flynn a-hugging third.
Then from five thousand throats and more there rose a lusty yell;
It rumbled in the mountaintops, it rattled in the dell;
It knocked upon the hillside and recoiled upon the flat,
For Casey, mighty Casey, was advancing to the bat.
There was ease in Casey's manner as he stepped into his place;
There was pride in Casey's bearing and a smile on Casey's face.
And when, responding to the cheers, he lightly doffed his hat,
No stranger in the crowd could doubt 'twas Casey at the bat.
Ten thousand eyes were on him as he rubbed his hands with dirt;
Five thousand tongues applauded when he wiped them on his shirt.
Then while the writhing pitcher ground the ball into his hip,
Defiance gleamed in Casey's eye, a sneer curled Casey's lip.
And now the leather-covered sphere came hurtling through the air,
And Casey stood a-watching it in haughty grandeur there.
Close by the sturdy batsman the ball unheeded sped –
'That ain't my style,' said Casey – 'Strike one,' the Umpire said.
From the benches black with people, there went up a muffled roar,

Like the beating of the storm-waves on a stern and distant shore.
'Kill him! kill the umpire!' shouted someone on the stand;
And it's likely they'd have killed him had not Casey raised his hand.
With a smile of Christian charity great Casey's visage shone;
He stilled the rising tumult; he bade the game go on;
He signalled to the pitcher, and once more the spheroid flew;
But Casey still ignored it, and the Umpire said, 'Strike two.'
'Fraud!' cried the maddened thousands, and the echo answered,
   'Fraud!'
But one scornful look from Casey and the multitude was awed.
They saw his face grow stern and cold, they saw his muscles strain,
And they knew that Casey wouldn't let that ball go by again.
The sneer is gone from Casey's lip, his teeth are clenched in hate;
He pounds with cruel violence his bat upon the plate.
And now the pitcher holds the ball, and now he lets it go,
And now the air is shattered by the force of Casey's blow.
Oh, somewhere in this favored land the sun is shining bright;
The band is playing somewhere, and somewhere hearts are light,
And somewhere men are laughing, and somewhere children shout;
But there is no joy in Mudville – mighty Casey has struck out.

E. J. THRIBB

LINES ON THE DEATH OF
CHAIRMAN MAO

So.
Farewell then
Chairman Mao.

You are the
Last of the
Great revolutionary

Figures. You
And I
Had little in
Common

Except that
Like me
You were a poet.

Though how you
Found time
To write poems

In addition to
Running a
Country of
800 million people

Is baffling
Frankly.

E. J. THRIBB

IN MEMORIAM
UFFA FOX

Farewell then, salty dog!
You have gone to sail
With the immortal mariners
Like for example Sir Francis
Drake and Vasco da Gama.

Uffa Fox! That has always
Struck me as a strange sort
Of name. I have never
Known anyone called Uffa before.

But it suited you
With your tousled grey hair
And friendship with the Royalty.

I expect HRH Prince Philip
Will miss you at Cowes.

So long then me old hearty!
Uffa! Man o' the ocean wave!

It's never been something I
Could see the point of personally
Sailing I mean.
Still everyone to his own.

JOHN WILMOT, EARL OF ROCHESTER 1647–80

KING CHARLES II

Here lies our mutton-eating King
    Whose word no man relies on,
Who never said a foolish thing,
    Nor ever did a wise one.

HUMBERT WOLFE 1885–1940

You cannot hope
    to bribe or twist,
thank God! the
    British journalist.

But, seeing what
    the man will do
unbribed, there's
    no occasion to.

VICTORIA WOOD 1953–

SATURDAY NIGHT

Oh dear what can the matter be?
Eight o'clock at night on a Saturday
Tracey Clegg and Nicola Battersby
Coming to town double quick.

They rendezvous in front of a pillar
Tracey's tall like Jonathan Miller
Nicola's more like Guy the Gorilla
If Guy the Gorilla were thick.

Their hair's been done it's very expensive
Their use of mousse and gel is extensive
As weapons their heads would be classed as offensive
And put under some kind of ban.

They're covered in perfumes but these are misnomers
Nicola's scent could send dogs into comas
Tracey's kills insects and dustbin aromas
And also gets stains off the pan.

Chorus:
But it's their night out
It's what it's all about
Looking for lads
Looking for fun
A burger and chips with a sesame bun
They're in the mood
For a fabulous interlude
Of living it up
Painting the town
Drinking Bacardi and keeping it down
But it's all all right
It's what they do of a Saturday night.

Oh dear what can the matter be?
What can that terrible crunching and clatter be?
It's the cowboy boots of Nicola Battersby
Leading the way into town.

They hit the pub and Tracey's demeanour
Reminds you of a loopy hyena
They have sixteen gins and a rum and Ribena
And this is before they've sat down.

They dare a bloke from Surrey called Murray
To phone the police and order a curry
He gets locked up, it's a bit of a worry
But they won't have to see him again.

They're dressed to kill and looking fantastic
Tracey's gone for rubber and plastic
Nicola's dress is a piece of elastic
It's under a heck of a strain.

Chorus:
But it's their night out
It's what it's all about
Ordering drinks
Ordering cabs
Making rude gestures with doner kebabs
They're in the mood
For a fabulous interlude
Of weeing in parks
Treading on plants
Getting their dresses caught up in their pants
And it's all all right
It's what they do of a Saturday night.

Oh dear what can the matter be?
What can that terrible slurping and splatter be?
It's Tracey Clegg and Nicola Battersby
Snogging with Derek and Kurt.

They're well stuck in to heavyish petting
It's far too dark to see what you're getting
Tracey's bra flies off, how upsetting
And several people are hurt.

Oh dear, oh dear
Oh dear, oh dear

Oh dear what can the matter be?
What can that motheaten pile of old tatters be?
It's Tracey Clegg and Nicola Battersby
Getting chucked off the last Ninety-two.

With miles to go and no chance of hitching
And Nicola's boots have bust at the stitching
Tracey laughs and says what's the point bitching
I couldn't give a bugger, could you?

KIT WRIGHT 1944–

SERGEANT BROWN'S PARROT

Many policemen wear upon their shoulders
Cunning little radios. To pass away the time
They talk about the traffic to them, listen to the news.
And it helps them to Keep Down Crime.

But Sergeant Brown, he wears upon his shoulder
A tall green parrot as he's walking up and down
And all the parrot says is 'Who's-a-pretty-boy-then?'
'I am,' says Sergeant Brown.

BENJAMIN ZEPHANIAH 1958–

TALKING TURKEYS!!

Be nice to yu turkeys dis christmas
Cos turkey jus wanna hav fun
Turkeys are cool, turkeys are wicked
An every turkey has a Mum.
Be nice to yu turkeys dis christmas,
Don't eat it, keep it alive,
It could be yu mate an not on yu plate
Say, Yo! Turkey I'm on your side.

I got lots of friends who are turkeys
An all of dem fear christmas time,
Dey wanna enjoy it, dey say humans destroyed it
An humans are out of dere mind,
Yeah, I got lots of friends who are turkeys
Dey all hav a right to a life,
Not to be caged up an genetically made up
By any farmer an his wife.

Turkeys jus wanna play reggae
Turkeys jus wanna hip-hop
Can yu imagine a nice young turkey saying,
'I cannot wait for de chop'?
Turkeys like getting presents, dey wanna watch christmas TV,
Turkeys hav brains an turkeys feel pain
In many ways like yu an me.

I once new a turkey called Turkey
He said 'Benji explain to me please,
Who put de turkey in christmas
An what happens to christmas trees?'
I said, 'I am not too sure turkey
But it's nothing to do wid Christ Mass
Humans get greedy an waste more dan need be
An business men mek loadsa cash.'

Be nice to yu turkey dis christmas
Invite dem indoors fe sum greens
Let dem eat cake an let dem partake
In a plate of organic grown beans,
Be nice to yu turkey dis christmas
An spare dem de cut of de knife,
Join Turkeys United an dey'll be delighted
An yu will mek new friends '**FOR LIFE**'.

ACKNOWLEDGEMENTS

— ◇ —

The publishers gratefully acknowledge the following for permission to reproduce copyright poems in this book. Every effort has been made to trace copyright holders, but in a few cases this has proved impossible. The publishers would be interested to hear from any copyright holders not here acknowledged.

13. 'Coffee in Heaven' from *From the Devil's Pulpit* (Bloodaxe Books, 1997) by John Agard, by kind permission of John Agard c/o Caroline Sheldon Literacy Agency.

14. 'Please Mrs Butler' from *Please Mrs Butler* by Allan Ahlberg (Kestrel Books, 1983). Copyright © Allan Ahlberg 1983.

25, 26. 'Give Me a Doctor' and 'Note on Intellectuals' from *Shorts, Collected Poems* by W.H. Auden. Reprinted by permission of Faber and Faber Ltd.

27, 29. 'Sling Another Chair Leg on the Fire, Mother' and 'Oh, I Wish I'd Looked After Me Teeth' from *The Works* by Pam Ayres, published by BBC Books. © Copyright Pam Ayres 1992.

33. 'It's a Great Big Shame'. Words by Edgar Bateman. Copyright 1895 Francis, Day and Hunter Ltd, WC2H 0EA. Reproduced by permission of International Music Publications Ltd.

35. 'A red sky at night' from *Old Surrey Saws and Sayings* by Sir Max Beerbohm. Copyright the Estate of Max Beerbohm, reprinted by permission of Berlin Associates.

36, 38, 39, 40, 41. 'Matilda ...', 'Rebecca ...' 'Henry King ...', 'Lord Finchley', 'The Frog' from *Complete Verse* by Hilaire Belloc, published by Random House UK Ltd. Reprinted by permission of The Peters Fraser and Dunlop Group Ltd on behalf of: *The Estate of Hilaire Belloc*. © Estate of Hilaire Belloc.

42. 'Clerihews' by E.C. Bentley. Reproduced with permission of Curtis Brown Ltd, London, on behalf of the Estate of E.C. Bentley. Copyright E.C. Bentley.

44, 45, 47. 'How to Get On in Society', 'A Subaltern's Love-song' and 'Hunter Trials' from *Collected Poems* by John Betjeman. Reprinted by permission of John Murray (Publishers) Ltd.

49. 'Ducks Don't Shop in Sainsburys' by Gary Boswell. First published in *It's Brilliant* (Stride, 1987). Later reproduced in *Toughie Toffee* (Collins, 1989) and *The Much Better Story Book* (Red Fox, 1992). Reprinted with kind permission of Stride Publications.

64. 'Bloody Men' from *Serious Concerns* by Wendy Cope. Reprinted by permission of Faber and Faber Ltd.

65. 'Lonely Hearts' from *Making Cocoa for Kingsley Amis* by Wendy Cope. Reprinted by permission of Faber and Faber Ltd.

66, 68. 'nobody loses all the time' and 'may i feel said he' are reprinted from *Complete Poems 1904–1962*, by E.E. Cummings, edited by George J. Firmage, by permission of W.W. Norton & Company. Copyright © 1991 by the Trustee for the E.E. Cummings Trust and George James Firmage.

70, 71, 74. 'St Ives', 'Hot and Cold' and 'A Hand in the Bird' from *Rhyme Stew* by Roald Dahl, published by Jonathan Cape and Penguin. Reprinted by permission of David Higham Associates.

72. 'Little Red Riding Hood and the Wolf' from *Revolting Rhymes* by Roald Dahl, published by Jonathan Cape and Penguin. Reprinted by permission of David Higham Associates.

75. 'Alternative Endings to an Unwritten Ballad' by Paul Dehn. Copyright the Estate of Paul Dehn, reprinted by permission of Berlin Associates.

77. 'Tullynoe: Tête-à-Tête in the Parish Priest's Parlour' from *A Snail in My Prime* by Paul Durcan. Reprinted by permission of The Blackstaff Press.

78. 'The Lion and Albert'. Words by George Marriott Edgar. Copyright 1933 Francis, Day and Hunter Ltd, London WC2H 0EA. Reproduced by permission of International Music Publications Ltd.

81, 83. 'Bustopher Jones: The Cat About Town' and 'Macavity: The Mystery Cat' from *Old Possum's Book of Practical Cats* by T.S. Eliot. Reprinted by permission of Faber and Faber Ltd.

85. 'The Black Box' by Gavin Ewart. First published in *The Deceptive Grin of the Gravel Porters* (*The London Magazine*, 1968). Reprinted by permission of Margo Ewart.

86. 'The Hippopotamus Song'. Words by Michael Flanders, music by Donald Swann. Copyright 1952 Chappell Music Ltd, Warner/Chappell Music Ltd, London W6 8BS. Reprinted by permission of International Music Publications Ltd. All rights reserved.

93. 'Stately as a Galleon' from *Stately as a Galleon* by Joyce Grenfell, published by Macmillan. © Joyce Grenfell 1978. Reprinted by permission of Shiel Land Associates Ltd.

95. 'Malcolm' from *Five Sugars Please* by John Hegley, published by Methuen Publishing Limited. Copyright © 1993 by John Hegley.

96, 97. 'In the Arms of My Glasses' and 'A Comparison of Logs and Dogs' from *Can I Come Down Now Dad?* by John Hegley, published by Methuen (1991). Reprinted by permission of The Peters Fraser and Dunlop Group Limited on behalf of John Hegley. © John Hegley.

98. 'Old Sam'. Words by Stanley Holloway. Copyright 1932 Francis, Day and Hunter Ltd, WC2H 0EA. Reprinted by permission of International Music Publications Ltd.

100. 'The Shades of Night' by A.E. Housman. Reprinted by permission of The Society of Authors as the Literary Representative of the Estate of A.E. Housman.

102. 'The Common Cormorant' from *Exhumations* by Christopher Isherwood. Reproduced with permission of Curtis Brown Ltd, London, on behalf of the Estate of Christopher Isherwood. Copyright the Estate of Christopher Isherwood.

103. 'The Book of My Enemy Has Been Remaindered' from *Other Passports* by Clive James, published by Jonathan Cape/Picador. Reprinted by permission of The Peters Fraser and Dunlop Group Ltd.

105. 'Warning' from *Selected Poems* by Jenny Joseph, published by Bloodaxe Books (1992). Reprinted by permission of John Johnson Ltd.

119, 120, 121. 'Cake', 'Stink' and 'Survivor' from *Selected Poems 1967–1987* by Roger McGough, published by Jonathan Cape (1989). Reprinted by permission of The Peters Fraser and Dunlop Group Limited on behalf of Roger McGough. © Roger McGough 1989.

122. 'Bagpipe Music' from *Collected Poems* by Louis MacNeice, published by Faber and Faber Ltd. Reprinted by permission of David Higham Associates.

124, 126. 'On the Ning Nang Nong' and 'Bump!' from *Silly Verse for Kids* by Spike Milligan, published by Puffin Books (1968). Reprinted by permission of Spike Milligan Productions Ltd.

125. 'Father Thames' from *Hidden Words* by Spike Milligan, published by Michael Joseph (1993). Reprinted by permission of Spike Milligan Productions Ltd.

127. 'The King's Breakfast' from *When We Were Very Young* © Copyright under the Berne Convention. Published by Egmont Books Limited, London and used with permission.

130. 'Celia Celia' from *Heart on the Left: Poems 1953–1984* by Adrian Mitchell, published by Bloodaxe Books (1997). Reprinted by permission of The Peters Fraser and Dunlop Group Limited on behalf of Adrian Mitchell. © Adrian Mitchell. Educational Health Warning! Adrian Mitchell asks that none of his poems are used in connection with any examinations whatsoever.

131. 'Just in Case' from *Poems in My Pocket* by Charlotte Mitchell, published by Souvenir Press (1991).

134, 135. 'Song of the Open Road' and 'Curl Up and Diet' from *Candy is Dandy* by Ogden Nash, published by Andre Deutsch Ltd (1983).

137. 'One Perfect Rose' from *The Collected Dorothy Parker* by Dorothy Parker. Reprinted by permission of Gerald Duckworth & Co. Ltd.

138. 'Hair Today, No Her Tomorrow' from *Storm Damage*, published by Flamingo, an imprint of HarperCollins. © Brian Patten, 1988. Reproduced by permission of the author c/o Rogers, Coleridge & White Ltd, 20 Powis Mews, London W11 1JN.

142. 'Chocolate Cake' from *Quick Let's Get Out of Here* by Michael Rosen, first published by Andre Deutsch Children's Books, an imprint of Scholastic Ltd. © Michael Rosen, 1983.

147. 'The Cremation of Sam McGee' from *Collected Verse* by Robert W. Service. Reprinted by permission of Iris Davies.

156, 157. 'Lines on the death of Chairman Mao' and 'In Memoriam Uffa Fox' by E.J. Thribb. Reprinted by permission of *Private Eye*.

159. 'You cannot hope ...' from *The Uncelestial City* by Humbert Wolfe, published by Gollancz (1930). Reprinted by permission of Miss Ann Wolfe.

160. 'Saturday Night' from *Lucky Bag* by Victoria Wood, published by Methuen.

163. 'Sergeant Brown's Parrot' from *Rabbiting On and Other Poems* by Kit Wright, published by HarperCollins. © Kit Wright.

164. 'Talking Turkeys!!' from *Talking Turkeys* by Benjamin Zephaniah (Viking, 1994). © Benjamin Zephaniah. Reproduced by permission of Penguin Books Ltd.

INDEX OF POETS' NAMES

— ◇ —

INDEX OF FIRST LINES

— ◇ —

W

Y